Knowledge is Power: A logical meaning of life

Sei Lebese

Published by Sei Lebese, 2020.

KNOWLEDGE IS POWER: A LOGICAL MEANING OF LIFE

First edition. March 18, 2020.

Written by Sei Lebese.

KNOWLEDGE
IS
POWER
A LOGICAL MEANING OF
LIFE

SEI LEBESE

ACKNOWLEDGEMENTS

My heartfelt thanks to Dr. Shakir Osman and his daughter Mrs Aashi Navuluri for editing this book. A special gratitude also goes to Dr Mafa Maiketso who introduced me to NUL Writing Club, without you, this piece of the book wouldn't have seen any light of the day. Lastly but not least importantly, many thanks to my family and teachers from primary level to tertiary level; your words of encouragement and appreciation have helped in making the publication of this work a reality.

PREFACE

There's only one possibility. You're wasting your irreplaceable time chasing meaningless goals, and when you die not only will your existence have been in vain but so will all the painful trials and tribulations you've worked so hard to overcome. Therefore, until you know the meaning of life the most important (the only important) thing you can be doing is trying to answer the question, "What is the meaning of life?"

Of course, it's easy to say you need to know the meaning of life, but if it were that easy to figure it out then we'd all know it already...but we don't. Why is that? Does the mere fact that there isn't a widely accepted answer prove the question is too difficult for us to answer? Or even worse, does it prove life has no meaning?

History shows that if we haven't done something it' rarely because we can't. It's just that we've been doing it wrong, and all the problem we once believed impossible were (or will be) solved the same way: through the proper use of logic. This problem is no different. The only way to understand the meaning of life is, and always has been, through the use of logic.

CHAPTER 1
THE VALUE OF LIFE

"A man who dares to waste on hour of time has not discovered the value of life." ~*Charles Darwin*

"Believe that life is worth living, and your belief will help create that fact." ~*William James*

Imagine yourself sitting on a park bench when a cute little girl walks up to you and demands that you explain everything she needs to know in life right there on the spot. If you choose not to dodge the responsibility by throwing a logic-stopping escape clause at her where would you begin explaining life?

I've relived that scenario in my head a million times, and I still question whether or not I have the right answer, but you have to draw a line in the sand at some point. So here's what I decided the first thing a young person should know about life is.

The amount of effort you put into anything you do depends on your motivation, and your motivation depends on understanding the importance of the goal you're trying to accomplish. For example, if someone offered you R1.00 to run across the continent you wouldn't do it. However, if someone offered you 1 Million Rands or told you they'd kill you and your whole family if you didn't then you'd certainly do it. You wouldn't even have to debate with yourself about it or work up the strength. Your motivation would be so strong there wouldn't be a choice. There would only be one path in front of you.

Think about how that applies to life in general. If you don't know why life is important or how important life is then you won't have the proper motivation to take life as seriously as you should. Thus you won't put the appropriate amount of effort into living. Instead your motivation and priorities will default to immediate, shortsighted, petty, and ultimately meaningless goals, and you'll squander the short time you have here on such trivialities. However, if you truly, truly, truly understand the value of life you won't have to debate with yourself or work up the strength to sacrifice the petty temptations of the world to pursue life's highest purpose. Your motivation would be so strong there'd only be one choice, one path before you. So the first lesson you need to learn about life is how valuable it is and why.

In order to explain the value of life we need to start from the very beginning, which was about billions years ago when all the matter and energy in the universe was compacted into an infinitely dense point in space called a singularity.

There's a lot we don't yet know about the singularity. We don't know why it was there or how it got there. We don't know whether it had existed forever or if it appeared out of nothing in a specific instant in time. For that matter we don't know if time or space existed back then in the same way we experience it today. There are theories that it probably didn't. All we've been able to reasonably deduce is that the singularity was there, and in an instant an unknown catalyst caused it (and possibly time and space) to expand to cosmic proportions. This event is commonly known as the Big Bang though the word "bang" may be a misnomer. "The Big Expansion" is often said to be more accurate.

Spending your entire life on this planet it's easy to take yourself for granted while perceiving the beautiful nebulas and globular clusters in the sky as miraculous celestial bodies, but look at earth from their point of view. You're a celestial body too. In fact, you're even more amazing than the most beautiful astronomical phenomenon. The fact that you, a sentient being, aware of your own existence and capable of self-determination, arose from inanimate matter is as miraculous as The Big Expansion itself.

The contradictory nature of your existence raises some more penetrating questions. We don't know why the universe exists at all, but we know that the physical universe is meticulously, mathematically, and consistently designed and behave according to fixed, unwavering rules. Why and how is it that these rules exist? How is it that those rules allowed for the sublimation of living creatures whose bodies are meticulously, mathematically, and consistently designed? Why is heredity mathematically predictable? Chance isn't predictable. So evolution must not be entirely the product of chance. If that's true then what else could it be the product of?

It's been theorized that the universe could have been designed by some form of intelligence. There's no conclusive evidence to back this theory up, but it's not entirely without precedent. After all, we ourselves are intelligent beings who arose from inanimate matter. And in a universe where you can't get something from nothing it would explain where our intelligence came from. Granted, that still leaves the issue of where the creator came from, which is no small question. Maybe the Creator existed forever. Of course, if He did then maybe the universe existed forever as well, but if that were the case then the universe wouldn't have needed a creator to create it since it was always there.

You can see where speculating about a creator will get you. So we won't get any further into that for now other than to point out one implication that arises from the existence of a creator. If there was logical intent behind your creation then your life has an extra source of value. You're valuable to the one who went through billions years of deliberate, calculated work creating you.

Regardless of whether or not your parents were the only intelligent beings responsible for bringing you to life there still aren't words to fully describe how cosmically epic in scale your existence is. And yet for all the work and purpose that went into bringing you here you'll only have a handful of decades to be a witness to yourself and all of creation. In a universe where time appears to be infinite you'll take a finite number of breaths. You'll speak a finite number of words. You'll see a finite number of blades of grass. You'll meet a finite number of people. Every moment of your life that ticks by was the only chance in all of eternity for you to experience that moment. That makes every moment of your life (no matter how mundane it may seem) infinitely rare and thus infinitely valuable. That makes every moment of your life the best moment of your life.

Despite the infinite value of life, someday you'll die. Why? What happens after we die? We don't know. We make up explanations about death that make us feel better about it, but the truth of the matter is you don't get to decide what happens after you die. What you believe doesn't change or prove anything. The only thing believing in an after-death scenario proves is you're too weak and afraid to admit your ignorance. You may think you're doing yourself a favor by creating an explanation to hide from your fears behind, but ultimately all your self-serving fantasies really accomplish is misleading you in life. Simply putting off worrying about death until the last minute isn't going to help you either because you won't be able to make the most out of life until you work through the stages of grief over your own mortality. Only then will you be able to soberly accept that you're going to die and get on with making the most of the time you have left in a logical, conscious way. In order to accomplish all of those things the wisest course of action is to just admit your ignorance and work within the parameters of the unknown.

The truth is we don't know what happens after we die. If the simplest answer is the correct one then our consciousness simply turns off and we cease to exist. If that's true then we need to ask ourselves, what effect does death have on the value of life? Does it render our lives meaningless? Does it matter what we do in life? Does it mean there are no consequences to our actions?

These are all logical concerns, but the evidence points to the conclusion that our situation isn't as grim as it might first appear. We've already established that we exist for an infinitely valuable reason, and what little time we have in life is infinitely valuable. Death doesn't change that. The value of one moment isn't effected by anything that happens (or doesn't happen) afterwards. Furthermore, you don't have to wait until after death to find consequences for our actions. You can call this "the rule of immediate karma." The decisions you make and the actions you perform at any given moment shape your experiences immediately. If you fill your life with anger, hatred, pettiness, etc. then that's what you're going to experience in those fleeting, irreplaceable moments of your infinitely valuable existence. It doesn't matter if you're not punished for it later because you already suffered the consequences of an infinitely negative nature the moment you did it. On the other hand, logical, positive behavior rewards itself immediately in an infinitely valuable way.

That's what is on the line. So given the infinitely rare chance to exist and be aware of your own existence. And given the epic scale of miraculous work that went into creating you. And given the fact that there is an infinitely valuable purpose for your existence. And given the possibility that you were created intentionally by an intelligent agent. And given the fleeting amount of time you have to fulfill your purpose in this universe. And given the fact that how you live your life has infinite consequences regardless of whether or not there's an afterlife, the most important thing you can be doing with your life right now is asking yourself. What's the most important thing I can be doing with my life?

CHAPTER 2

THE MEANING OF LIFE

"The great and glorious masterpiece of humanity is to know how to live with a purpose." ~Montaigne

"For most of human history we have searched for our place in the cosmos. Who are we? What are we? We find that we inhabit an insignificant planet of a hum-drum star lost in a galaxy tucked away in some forgotten corner of a universe in which there are far more galaxies than people. We make our world significant by the courage of our questions, and by the depth of our answers." ~Carl Sagan

If you don't know the meaning of life then you can't be consciously working towards fulfilling it. If you're not working towards fulfilling the sole purpose for which you exist then you need to ask yourself, what are you doing with your life?

So let's break the problem down logically. Think of the question, "What is the meaning of life?" as an equation. Now, you can't solve an equation without knowing the variables, and if you change the variables in any equation you create a whole new equation with a new answer. This means you can't just ask, "What's the meaning of life?" because there are no variables in that equation to work with. It's like asking, "What's the answer to the question?" You need to identify the variables in order to finish the question, which should really be stated, "What is the meaning of life if..."

The three dots at the end of that sentence represent another reason we've had a hard time answering the question. We can't agree on how to finish stating the question because we can't agree on the variables.

In the equation of the meaning of life the two most important variables are also the least agreed upon. They're how the universe came into existence and what happens after we die. In other words, God and the afterlife. These are the keys to solving the problem since they explain the creation of life and our destiny afterwards, both of which entail and imply why we're here.

If we're ever going to understand the meaning of life we have to come to a conclusion about whether or not God or an afterlife exists. Unfortunately, the reason nobody can agree on whether or not God or an afterlife exists is because we can't prove or disprove either possibility.

How can we get past this dilemma? As always, the answer is logic. If all the variables in this equation are equal then we should give each variable equal consideration.

In order to do that we have to break the question, "What is the meaning of life if...?" into four separate questions, each with different variables, and therefore with potentially different answers:

1. What is the meaning of life if there is no God and no afterlife?

2. What is the meaning of life if there is a God but no afterlife?

3. What is the meaning of life if there is no God but there is an afterlife?

4. What is the meaning of life if there is a God and an afterlife?

The next seven chapters of this book analyze these four scenarios objectively to deduce what the meaning of life could be under each set of conditions. The rest of the book analyzes how to fulfill the meaning of life. The reason it takes seven chapters to answer four questions is because both the questions and the answers overlap each other. For example, if there's a God then there are some things that'll be the same regardless of whether or not there's an afterlife. So to avoid repetition and make everything easier to understand the information will be presented in this order:

1. Why are we here if God does not exist regardless of whether or not there is an afterlife?

2. What if God does not exist and there is no afterlife?

3. What if God does not exist and there is an afterlife?

4. Why are we here if God does exist regardless of whether or not there is an afterlife?

5. What if God exists and there is no afterlife?

6. what if God exits and there is an afterlife?

7. What is the same regardless of whether or not God exists or whether or not there is an afterlife?

CHAPTER 3
WHY ARE WE HERE IF GOD DOESN'T EXIST?

"I believe in God, only I spell it Nature." ~Frank Lloyd Wright

"The idea that God is an oversized white male with a flowing beard who sits in the sky and tallies the fall of every sparrow is ludicrous. But if by 'God' one means the set of physical laws that govern the universe, and then clearly there is such a God. This God is emotionally unsatisfying... it does not make much sense to pray to the law of gravity." ~Carl Sagan

There's no irrefutable proof that God exists. Therefore it's logical to conclude that He doesn't. People have tried to side step this inconvenient fact by asking the trick question, "If God didn't create the universe then who did?"

If the universe wasn't created by a sentient divinity then there are only two possible ways to explain its existence. One, it has existed forever. Two, it created itself. Ironically, it'd take an equal amount of faith to believe that God either created Himself or has existed forever. Actually, given that all of these possibilities are equal and there's no proof of God's existence this trick question actually lends more credibility to the possibility that the universe either created itself or has existed forever.

REVERSE ENGINEERING THE UNIVERSE

If there's no God then the physical universe is all that exists. So we only have the physical universe to look to for proof of the meaning of life. So let's analyze the universe and see what clues it holds.

We know this much: the laws of nature don't change, and the universe behaves according to math. Let's analyze these two facts and see what we can deduce from them.

Consider that the laws of nature don't change or make mistakes. If you study the laws of nature you'll always find yourself studying predictable patterns. Every molecule adheres to the same fundamental rules all the time, everywhere.

It can be argued that electrons and antimatter behave randomly, but even if that's true the laws of nature that control their movements don't. They won't switch to behaving predictability for no reason. So the laws controlling the universe are still consistent.

If the entire universe behaves with such perfect precision it'd be inconsistent and therefore impossible for the universe to have come into existence on accident. Furthermore, if the behavior of all the matter in the universe adheres to inherent, fixed formulas, and life forms are made from that same matter, then it would be equally inconsistent and thus impossible for the surfacing of life in the universe to have been an accident as well. The potential for matter to form into living organisms must be as much an inherent trait of atoms as it is for them to form into a solid, liquid, or gas under the right conditions.

Both of these observations advocate that our existence isn't an accident. If it's true that we're not an accident then there must be a reason why we're here. After all, every cause has an effect, and every effect has a cause. If our existence is the effect then we must have had a cause, and there must be a reason why the whole cause and effect chain of events that brought us here was set in motion in the first place. Without a reason it couldn't and wouldn't have happened.

We can begin to deduce the reason for our creation by analyzing the fact that the universe is mathematical in nature. It's been said that math is the language of science because everything that happens in nature on an atomic level is the product of mathematical equations: chemical reactions, gravitational pull, temperature changes, etc. So if every event in nature happens the way it does because it's the solution to a mathematical equation then the creation of the universe, and later the creation of life, must have also been solutions to mathematical equations. Thus, it's easy to say that on the most basic level we exist because it's a mathematical truth that we should exist.

THE MISSING CLOCK MAKER

Without a God to solve that mathematical equation we're simply the product of the equation, period. Now, some of you might be wondering, "If God wasn't there to ask the question then who asked it?"

Does anyone ask how many electrons an atom should gain or lose when it comes into contact with another atom? Does anyone ask how fast light should travel? Doesn't two plus two still equal four even if nobody is there to ask it? If the universe began at a specific instant in time wouldn't math and potential still have existed before anything else did? The answer to all of those questions seems to be, "Yes." The forces of nature don't need a voice. Math doesn't need a voice, and neither does truth. These things are intangible, eternal, and exist independent of anything else.

Some of you may now be thinking, "Even if nobody needed to ask the question somebody still needed to make the solution a reality."

Not if truth is reality.

THE MOTIVES OF THE MACHINE

The next logical question for us to ask is, if we exist because it's a mathematical truth that we should exist then why is it a mathematical truth that we should exist?

You can narrow down the answer to that question by taking us out of the equation. What if we didn't exist? What would be the consequence if all forms of life suddenly disappeared?

Nothing! Absolutely nothing would be affected. The planets would still spin obediently around their stars. Galaxies would continue to float across space on their course to oblivion or the Big Crunch, and all the rocks and gas wouldn't notice a difference.

The only thing that would be affected by our disappearance would be us. So if the existence of life doesn't serve any external purpose in the universe then the only value life has is to the living. So we must have been made for us.

Now, if the laws of nature alone are responsible for creating us then does that mean the universe is benevolent and gave us life out of the kindness of its...computation? That's one possibility, but there's a more logical one.

You see, the idea that the universe is here to serve us assumes that we're above it, but we aren't above it. We're a part of it. We're made of atoms just like everything else. So it's more logical that the universe didn't create us for us; it didn't give us life as a gift. Instead it gave itself life. We're just an extension of the universe. We're the universe incarnate. The reason why we exist isn't because it's true that we should be alive. Rather the reason why we exist is because it's true that the universe should be alive.

If the universe's goal was just to be alive it could have settled with manifesting itself as plants. There'd be a lot less bloodshed that way. Yet here you are. You're proof that the universe was aiming for something more than just life. Its goal was to be at least what you are: sentient, awake, aware, conscious. The universe calculated that it's good to be self-aware and be able to make decisions, to have a free will, to own an identity, a personality, a mind. To be someone. So the meaning of life isn't just "to be." Nor is it just to be alive. It's to be someone.

Maybe someday we'll evolve into more amazing beings and find that the universe had something even more ambitious in mind, but that doesn't negate our lives right now, and it doesn't mean the meaning of life is just to breed. The universe is awake right now and is seeking to experience the fullness of being awake. The meaning of life is to fulfill the goal of experiencing being.

CHAPTER 4

WHAT IF GOD DOESN'T EXIST AND THERE IS NO AFTERLIFE?

"I have never seen the slightest scientific proof of the religious theories of heaven and hell, of future life for individuals, or of a personal God."~ Thomas Edison

"I would love to believe that when I die I will live again, that some thinking, feeling, remembering part of me will continue. But as much as I want to believe that, and despite the ancient and worldwide cultural traditions that assert an afterlife, I know of nothing to suggest that it is more than wishful thinking." ~ Carl Sagan

It's logical that God doesn't exist because there's no proof of His existence. It's also logical to believe there's no afterlife for the same reason: because there's no proof. Nor is there proof of the existence of a soul that could survive death or any alternate spiritual universes for a soul to go to.

Some people say that absence of proof doesn't prove that something isn't true. That's debatable, but that doesn't matter, because in this case there actually is circumstantial evidence in the physical universe that suggests there isn't an afterlife.

Ancient Chinese philosophers noticed that the natural world (as well as human experiences) can be divided into two sides, Yin and Yang. Darkness and Light. Good and Bad. Creation and Destruction. And so on and so forth.

Likewise, modern scientists have found matter and anti-matter as well as negatively charged electrons and positively charged protons. An object is either in motion or it's at rest. Computer programming is based on the concept that a circuit is either on or off, and every vibrant thing you watch on television, hear on the radio, or see on the internet can be reduced to a stream of "1s" and "0s" or "ones" and "offs." Everything is either in a state of entropy or a state of equilibrium. Either way, the end result is the same: finality at one end of the spectrum. If we apply this concept to life and death we can see a compelling argument that in this kind of universe you're either alive or dead.

NO PAIN NO GAIN

But why give us life just to snatch it away from us after a handful of years? The answer is simple and scientific. Death is necessary to make room for our decedents to grow and evolve. If nothing had ever died your ancestors would still be here and you wouldn't. Wishing for a longer life is selfish. You're going to die for the greater good. Deal with it.

PLAYING THE HAND YOU'VE ALREADY WON

Regardless of whether or not there is in fact an afterlife, we should live life as there weren't because it's unsafe to assume there is. It makes us complacent. It gives us an excuse to put off living until after we die. It's more logical to err on the side of caution and assume we only have a short amount of time to live. That way we're motivated to make the most out of it. Therefore, what we should really be worrying about is what to do with the time we have here and now.

But why do anything? If we're all going to die anyway does it even matter what we do with our time?

Why not just spend our whole lives drowning our existential misery in booze and conciliating ourselves with the pleasures of the flesh until that fatal moment when this cruel, pointless charade finally ends?

There's a logical reason why, actually. The fact that we're all alone in the universe and only have a few moments to live can either be the most terrible or the most fantastic thing you ever hear depending on how you look at it. On one hand, the fleetingness of life means we're all on death row and nothing we ever do matters in the long run, but life only seems futile if we assume it's a means to an end. But what if your life isn't a means to an end? What if your life is justified because it's an end in and of itself?

Through you, the universe gave itself consciousness and a body to experience and enjoy life with. Everything that's happened up to this point could be a means to that end. That would mean when you ask yourself, "How do I fulfill the meaning of life?" you're not asking it as a person who's been alive for less than a hundred years. You're asking it as the eyes and ears of the universe. From that point of view you've personally been working on fulfilling the meaning of life since before the big bang, through the cooling of the galaxies and the formation or evolution of life. Simply by being born you've already fulfilled the meaning of life by 98%. You're fulfilling another 1% with every breath you take, because by and large the meaning of life is for you to be alive and experience existence. This means you don't have to wait until after you graduate, get a career, get married, have kids, retire, change the world, paint your masterpiece, or die before your life has meaning. You're there now.

There's just one little thing left to do: be you. If you're the universe incarnate, and you created you for you then you didn't create yourself to sit idly until death or to serve any external authority (be that a person, government, culture, ideology, or deity) in the meantime. You put yourself here to be a unique individual and exercise your free will to choose what you want to be and do...with a few probable exceptions.

First, hurting other incarnations of the universe would be counterproductive to all the work you've done to bring life into existence. Secondly, if you choose not to define yourself or your wants then there was little purpose in you being born in the first place. Finally, if you allow someone else to define your identity and your wants then your free will is wasted.

In order to make the most of your existence you need to become you to the fullest extent possible. Psychologists call this achieving self-actualization. Philosophers call it enlightenment. Parental guardians call it growing up. And this concept doesn't just apply to humans. It applies to all life. What does a plant accomplish in its life but grow to fulfill its potential as a plant? Animals are the same way. The difference between sentient beings such as us and every other living creature we know of is that we can choose what that potential is and how hard we're willing to work to achieve it.

CHAPTER 5

WHAT IF GOD DOESN'T EXIST AND THERE IS AN AFTERLIFE?

"There are no ordinary people... it is immortals whom we joke with, work with, marry, snub, and exploit."~ C.S. Lewis

"In death, I am born." ~Native American Proverb

If we can believe the unconscious forces of nature are powerful enough to give us life and take it away then it's reasonable to assume that an unconscious universe is also powerful enough to provide us with an afterlife, and it can be argued that there should be an afterlife because a mortal life is a waste of potential. It took trillions of years for conscious life to appear on Earth, and a person only gets to live for about a hundred years? The cost-benefit analysis doesn't seem to add up. From this point of view a mortal life is a waste of potential and it makes more sense that there should be an afterlife.

While there's definitely logic behind these ideas there's no empirical evidence to back them up. However, there may be circumstantial evidence in the natural universe to suggest that an afterlife exists.

If the universe began at a specific instant in time then there was a time when no physical matter existed but an intangible force real enough and powerful enough to give birth to the physical universe did exist. Even if the universe has existed forever there are still intangible laws that control the behavior of the universe. There are unseen hands at work. There's no telling what else is real that we can't see.

Probably the best argument for an afterlife though is that matter or energy can neither be created nor destroyed but only change forms. If that's true then the door to life could swing both ways as well. When we die our life isn't destroyed but merely changes form.

While there are logical arguments for the existence of an afterlife there are no logical arguments for what an afterlife would be like. There's no way to deduce if we'll remember who we are, if we'll have bodies, if we'll have wings, if we'll get to have sex, if our families will be with us, if we'll be reincarnated, etc. It's tempting to speculate about such fancies, but we should be honest with ourselves. We obviously can't know, and even what little we've deduced is still purely theoretical speculation.

THE EMPTY SEAT OF JUDGEMENT

Worst of all though, we don't know if we'll be judged for the things we've done in our mortal life. The only problem with that is...if there isn't a sentient being to watch or record our actions and subsequently decide or enforce our eternal fate then how could any of that happen?

Maybe we simply relive this life over and over again. Maybe we're reincarnated. Maybe our souls die if we're too weak to survive death. Maybe we have to spend eternity trapped in the mind we created while we were alive. Maybe the universe created a demigod to record our deeds and judge us. Maybe there's only one person in the universe and you have to experience life from everyone else's perspective one by one so we're blessed or condemned to experience the way we treat each other. Maybe there's only one person in the universe and each person is merely an eye that closes when that body dies. Any of these scenarios are just as likely as any others because there's no evidence in the universe to suggest how the afterlife works.

On one hand, this is evidence that there really isn't an afterlife to worry about, but on the other hand, all things being equal the safest route is to assume that there is an afterlife in which we'll be judged. We just don't know what standards we'll be judged by. In order to figure out what we're supposed to do while we're here we need to figure out what the meaning of life is.

When you ask, "What is the meaning of life?" notice you're not asking what the meaning of human life is. Grammatically you're asking why all life exists. From this point of view we're not "above" any other life form. We're simply another life form. The best we can say about ourselves is that we're more complicated. All things live. All things die, and if one living thing has a soul then all living things have souls. If our destiny is the same as plants and animals then our obligations are the same as well.

The best a plant or animal can aspire to do is grow to its full potential. The same is true of us. The difference between us and the rest of our plant and animal brethren is that we have the obligation to fulfill our mind's potential as well as our physical potential.

As for the moral rules we should follow (regardless of whether they have any effect on the afterlife), if the rest of the universe operates according to math then so should we. This means all our moral codes should be based on logic, and in order to be moral you need to develop your ability to reason. If you follow any rules blindly without coming to those conclusions logically then you may be gambling with the fate of your soul. Plus, you make yourself a slave to those rules and to the person who gave you those rules, and you weren't given life to become a willing slave. That's a waste of your potential and might even stunt the growth of your soul to the extent that it won't be strong enough to survive death. That or you might not deserve to survive death.

CHAPTER 6

WHY ARE WE HERE IF GOD EXISTS?

"I cannot imagine how the clockwork of the universe can exist without a clockmaker." ~ Voltaire

"If you don't know what's meant by God, watch a forsythia branch or a lettuce leaf sprout." ~ Martin H. Fischer

It's logical that God exists, and the most compelling evidence of His existence is evolution. This shouldn't be confused with natural selection. Natural selection does a good job of explanation how chance genetic mutations will give the offspring of one organism an advantage or disadvantage over the offspring of the organisms around it, but it doesn't do a good job of explaining the process by which a living thing evolved from inanimate matter to a single celled organism to a multi celled organism to its final state complete with environment-tailored natural defenses, reproductive capabilities, a brain, interworking organ systems, complicated sensory receptors, and especially a taxonomic rank in a systematically interconnected kingdom of life.

ANOTHER TRIP ON THE BEAGLE

The reason natural selection doesn't do a good job of explaining that process is because when you talk about life you rarely find yourself talking about accidents. Remember, life itself didn't emerge in the universe on accident. The fact that all life can be arranged in a logical taxonomical order points to order, not accident. It's unlikely that sunflowers, starfish, and sea shells contain geometric patterns on accident. It's also unlikely that dogs have eyes, birds have tongues, plants process energy, and bacteria reproduce, all of which humans have or do also. If every living thing is a chance mutation then why are we all still so similar?

Look at the human body. Do you think it's an accident that the left and right sides are symmetrical? Thousands of intellectual geniuses have been designing computers for decades but have failed to create one anywhere near as advanced as the human brain. We can't produce energy generators or waste processors as compact and efficient as the human body. We don't have video cameras as advanced as our eyes or sound systems as advanced as our ears. If our bodies are designed more intelligently than any machine we've been able to build then is it truly logical to say our bodies were designed by random trial and error? Or does it make more sense that our evolution progressed in a more orderly fashion than that?

If evolution wasn't orderly we couldn't make any successful predictions about heredity. DNA is blatantly mathematical. The way researchers hope to identify intelligent extraterrestrial life is by finding a transmission (be it radio, light, etc.) that contains some kind of mathematical pattern that couldn't happen randomly in nature. Well, our DNA is a mathematical pattern that couldn't happen randomly in nature.

The type of evolution that can bridge the gap between a single celled organism and intelligent life requires DNA to change so intelligently and purposefully that it almost seems like our DNA can learn, think, and plan.

There are two ways to explain this phenomenon. One, the original single celled organism we evolved from already contained the complete blueprint of what it would evolve into thousands of years later and it's just been fulfilling a predetermined plan throughout the course of its evolution. The other possibility is that DNA doesn't have a predetermined goal but calculates its changes as it goes along. That would mean our DNA behaves like a biological computer program...specifically, a self-replicating virus that can rewrite itself to adapt to its environment.

Whichever of those scenarios is true is irrelevant for the topic of hand. What's important is that in a scientific universe you can't get something from nothing. So if there's intelligence inherent in the evolution of our DNA then it had to come from a source that antedated it: an intelligent Creator (who either created Himself or has existed forever).

ASTRONAUT JELLYFISH

Not sold on the idea yet? Consider this analogy: A group of Earthling astronauts land on a distant planet. They scour the surface searching for living organisms but don't find any. However, they keep running across houses. So they know there was intelligent life on the planet at one time because precision built structures, such as houses, don't just occur randomly in nature. If you can agree with that logic then you should also be able to agree with the next part.

Imagine that a million years from now a group of jelly fish-like aliens come to earth in search of life. However, long before the aliens arrived in our galaxy humans had destroyed our atmosphere; all living things died, and the harsh environment tore down all the building humans had ever built.

So the aliens don't find any living creatures or buildings to deduce the existence of intelligent life from. However, they find some skeletons frozen in ice. Since the aliens are jelly fish-like creatures they don't recognize skeletons as the remains of living organisms. Nevertheless, they still use the skeletons to deduce that there was once intelligent life on planet Earth because a skeleton is proof of life for the same reason that houses are: skeletons are too precisely and consistently designed to happen randomly in nature. Of course, skeletons do happen in nature...but not randomly. It seems they must have been created by something intelligent.

ONLY ONE WAY TO LEARN HOW TO FLY

Unfortunately, we can't talk to God to find out why He went through all the trouble to create us. To make matters worse, it's generally accepted that humans can't know the mind of God and would be foolish to make assumptions. However, if we don't make any assumptions about the nature of God then it would be practically useless to believe in God because there would be nothing to believe in.

So let's venture a few basic assumptions about the nature of our creator. We can assume that He's infinitely powerful (or close enough), logical, and caring. We also know that we weren't created in His presence (at least in the sense that we can't interact with Him in the same way we interact with other people).

We can assume He's infinitely powerful (or close enough) because He created everything. He's logical because the universe He created is brilliantly mathematical. Finally, He cares about us, because it'd be illogical for Him to create or maintain all this and hate or even be disinterested in it.

With these variables we can deduce that God probably isn't a codependent parent or a slave driver who would punish us for not loving Him because that wouldn't very love, logical or efficient. If God wanted slaves He could have just created them instead of creating us in an exiled universe and giving us the ability to think and then turning around and telling us not to think but to serve Him or die. Telling someone "Do what I say or die." Isn't giving him a free choice. That's giving him an ultimatum to choose between slavery and murder.

If God is infinitely powerful then why would He create us? We can't do anything for Him that He can't do for Himself. This suggests that God didn't create us to benefit Him. But who else could benefit from us being alive? Us! God created us for us, which would fit the motive of an all loving parent.

Isn't that the ideal reason for having a child? You bring more life into existence and you do it as a gift and don't expect anything in return, and you still love and care for your children even if they don't love you or pay attention to you in return.

It doesn't take an infinitely logical being to come to the conclusion that the most logical motive for an infinitely loving God to create us is to give us life as a gift, a way of sending us out of the nest to become our own persons: to be, to live, to grow, to think, to choose, and to experience the majesty of existing as free people so that our lives may have value and meaning.

If you look at all the pain and suffering in the world you may come to the conclusion that God doesn't care about us. To add more evidence to this conclusion is the fact that God doesn't answer prayers or perform miracles.

A closer look at the evidence points back to the conclusion that God does care about us. Our lives may be more comfortable if God were to coddle us, but look at what happens when a parent coddles their children. The child grows up codependent and weak. They can't stand on their own and be their own person. So a loving parent has to let their children fall in order to learn how to walk. In the long run that's the most loving thing a parent can do, which is most likely why we were born in a this stoic universe where we stand or fall without God influencing the outcome either way.

CHAPTER 7

WHAT IF GOD EXISTS AND THERE IS NO AFTERLIFE?

"*The goal of all life is death.*" ~ Sigmund Freud

"*The fear of death follows from the fear of life. A man who lives fully is prepared to die at any time.*" ~ Mark Twain

It's usually taken for granted that the existence of God goes hand in hand with the existence of an afterlife, but there's no reason you can't have one without the other. In fact, the evidence suggests it. There's empirical evidence that God exists (evolution), but there no reliable evidence for an afterlife.

Look at the facts. God doesn't have a physical body. We do. We're completely separated. It's popular to believe that when we die that gap will be bridged, but there's no proof of that. Again, the only observable facts are that we're here, and He's there. That's the way it is, and that's probably how it's always going to be.

ON A DESERTED ISLAND LIFE STILL GOES ON

If there isn't an afterlife then in the end the believers and nonbelievers are all stuck in the same boat. When we die our consciousness ceases to exist. Thus, we cease to exist. So we need to figure out at as early an age possible what to do with the short time we have here.

Regardless of whether we were created by an unconscious universe or a sentient God the reasoning behind creation is still the same. We're here to experience being us to the fullest extent possible, and in order to accomplish that we need to grow in both mind and body as much as possible.

Furthermore, if God is infinitely logical then logic is God's way. So if we want to be religious we should mimic God and become logicians; to think illogically would be to act contrary to God's nature.

THE MISSING TIP JAR

There's only one more aspect of what we should do with our lives that needs to be clarified. Since we'll never meet God or be judged by

Him would it be immoral to act like He doesn't exist at all or should we acknowledge Him somehow? Should we feel obligated to thank Him? And if so then how?

Granted, in the end it doesn't matter if you thank God or not. The end result is the same, but if you do choose to thank God you have to ask yourself, what would an all-powerful, logical, and loving parent want? How would we even give thanks to a being we can't interact with?

The only thing we can deduce that God wants is for all of us to grow up and fulfill our potential. So if you want to thank God then you need to embark on a lifelong, systematic quest to do what you were put here for: to grow. If you want to take it a step further then help the rest of His representatives fulfill the meaning of life as well. And above all, don't hinder anyone from fulfilling their potential through physical or emotional violence, inaction, or using your socio-economic power to exploit and or oppress those with less power than you.

It seems illogical to devote our lives to talking to and praising God even if our intentions are sincere. Imagine if you sacrificed every other opportunity in your life to talk to and praise your parents for giving birth to you. They'd kick you out of their house and tell you you're wasting the life they worked so hard to give you. How much more annoyed and grieved God must be to see His children turn their backs on the purpose of their creation.

Suppose you have left your parents' house and made your own way in the world like you were supposed to. Now you're doing so well for yourself that you've got some extra money you'd like to give back to God to say thank you. You can't actually give the money to God directly, but there are a lot of people out there who claim to be "more" of a representative of God than you who would love to take your money.

First of all, there isn't any empirical evidence to suggest that anyone is any "more" of a representative of God than anyone else. Even if there were, giving your money to them wouldn't necessarily mean you're actually giving your money to God "more" than you would have if you'd given it to a starving or dying person. In fact, if that self-proclaimed representative of God spends one cent of that money on anything other than helping a starving or dying person then it'd be hard to argue that that money was truly given to God because it means that starving or dying person is in fact going to starve or die, which we've already deduced is obviously not what God wants. It's safe to conclude that anyone who spends God's money on temples is not a representative of God at all.

CHAPTER 8

WHAT IF THERE IS A GOD AND AN AFTERLIFE?

"I would rather live my life as if there is a God and die to find out there isn't, than live my life as if there isn't and die to find out there is."~ Albert Camus

"Belief is a wise wager. Granted that faith cannot be proved, what harm will come to you if you gamble on its truth and it proves false? If you gain, you gain all; if you lose, you lose nothing. Wager, then, without hesitation, that He exists." ~ Blaise Pascal

It's already been stated in earlier scenarios why it's logical that God can exist and why an afterlife can exist. Evolution is proof of God's existence, and life is wasted on death. We've also already seen how we can use the existence of an afterlife to deduce that souls exist and that this life is a birthing process for the next life. Furthermore, we don't know what happens in the afterlife or whether our actions in this life will affect us in the next. This uncertainty makes it logical to err on the side of caution and try to fulfill God's will as much as possible, which is done by growing to your full potential and helping others do the same.

There are only a few things that change in regards to the afterlife when we introduce God as a factor. Most importantly, this gives us more circumstantial evidence to suggest the existence of an afterlife. If God is immortal then a precedent has been set that sentient beings can be immortal too. If God doesn't have a physical body then a precedent has been set that humans don't need physical bodies. And the existence of God not only provides us with a source of power strong enough to provide us with an afterlife but also a loving God-parent who would possess the motives to usher us into the afterlife.

ARE THERE PUBLIC DEFENDENTS IN THE AFTERLIFE?

The only question left to ask is, what if we don't grow up? Will God punish us? First of all, a preoccupation with judgment misses the point of being alive. God gave us life for the most ideal, loving reasons a human parent gives birth to a child: to love him, watch him grow, and allow him to experience taking ownership of his own person. If we don't make the most of life then it's fair and logical that the worst that should happen to us is to miss out on the full potential of the afterlife to the extent that we missed out on the full potential of this life and nothing worse.

However, it's obvious even to children that it's illogical to give everybody different experiences in life and different amounts of time to live and expect the exact same results from everyone. Nobody knows what happens after death, but it seems illogical to believe that our souls are eternally and irrevocably judged and then atrociously punished immediately upon death by an infinitely logical and loving parent who generously went through a lot of trouble to create not only us but also an infinitely large and intricately designed universe for us to live in.

Here's another way to look at it. Ask yourself these questions: Did God create us because He was lonely? Did God create us so He could spend eternity "Lording" over us and rubbing it in our faces how inferior we are? Did God create us so we could eventually come back to Him and warm ourselves around his hearth fire and enjoy a rewarding family life in which we're not demoted to a servile status? Did God create us so that one day we could grow up into spiritual adults and look Him in the eye as a friend and companion (maybe even an equal)? Or did God create us so that we could eventually become superior to Him because we have free will and He doesn't?

How would eternal damnation help God accomplish any of those goals? It wouldn't. There's no conceivable use for eternal damnation except as a boogey man story for human adults to use to scare children (and other adults) into "behaving."

If you insist on being preoccupied with the judgment of your eternal soul then you should become preoccupied with fulfilling the meaning of life, which is growing to your full potential. If you want to go the extra mile you can devote your life to helping others fulfill their potential. Don't devote your life to prayer or ritual. God is taken care of. He doesn't need our attention. The people dying in the gutters need our attention. So grow, think, and help your brothers and sisters, and when you die you can confidently let the chips fall where they may.

CHAPTER 9
WHAT IF ALL OF THIS IS WRONG?

"Our greatest challenge today...is to couple conviction with doubt. By conviction, I mean some pragmatically developed faith, trust, or centeredness; and by doubt I mean openness to the ongoing changeability, mystery, and fallibility of the conviction." ~Kirk Schneider

"...convictions might be more dangerous enemies of the truth than lies."~ Friedrich Nietzsche

All of the scenarios just mentioned contradicted each other. That wasn't hypocritical or accidental. It was objective. However, in order to be truly objective we must also consider that all of these scenarios are wrong.

Each of the scenarios just mentioned involved an element of speculation. So far from simply being humble, it's entirely possible that all of the speculation was incorrect. Furthermore, if it's true that the simplest answer is usually the correct one then the most likely scenario is that we can't know the meaning of life. It may even be that life has no meaning.

Be that as it may, we're still here. Our lives are still infinitely valuable. We're still going to die, and we still need to figure out what to do with our short time here.

Throwing your hands up in the air and quitting isn't going to accomplish anything useful for yourself or your fellow man. Even with the vast amount of unknowns in life you still have a brain capable of thinking, and you can still use it to come to decide what the best thing to do with your life is under the circumstances. If you can't figure it out then that's you're first clue. The first and most important thing you need to do is improve your knowledge and thinking skills to the point where you can figure something out.

The difficulty in solving the question of what to do with life isn't how complicated it is but how simple it is. Look around you. What do you expect to do in this universe? Should you spend your life building something? Should you spend it earning money? Securing the love or fear of those who will die? Nothing you can do with your hands matters but in a fleeting, compartmentalized way.

Who you are still matters more than what you do. The universe you experience is defined by who you are. Your life is defined by who you are, and you are always you no matter where you go, what you do or what happens to you. Who you are matters more than anything else right now regardless of whether or not your life irrevocably ends tomorrow.

Who you are determined by who you've become. Who you've become is determined by how much effort you've put into creating yourself. Even if becoming yourself to the fullest potential isn't the meaning of life it's still the most important thing you can achieve in your life, and it's an essential prerequisite to being able to figure out the true meaning of life if that's even possible.

CHAPTER 10
WHAT REMAINS

"A musician must make music, an artist must paint, a poet must write, if he is to be ultimately at peace with himself. What a man can be, he must be."~ Abraham Maslow

"Those who improve with age embrace the power of personal growth and personal achievement and begin to replace youth with wisdom, innocence with understanding, and lack of purpose with self-actualization." Bo Bennett

"Self-awareness or self-consciousness can lead to the enlarging of consciousness. It can lead to the expansion of control of one's life. Self-awareness involves the capacity of not only looking back, but also looking ahead. Self-awareness is not only a gift, but it is a responsibility."~ Mufti James Hannush

The argument of whether or not God exits is moot. The same power was present at The Big Expansion. The real argument is whether or not that power was sentient. But even that doesn't matter, because in either case the intentions were the same.

The argument of whether or not there's an afterlife is equally moot. The safest route is to assume there isn't an afterlife so that we're motivated to make the most out of the short time we have here. At the same time though, the safest route is to assume there is an afterlife where we'll be judged so we're motivated to figure out the right way to live. So the safest route is to hope for the best and plan for the worst.

Also, if there's no afterlife then the short time we have to live is infinitely important. However, if our actions determine the quality of an infinitely long afterlife then our actions today are infinitely important. No matter which of scenario you choose to believe in, even if you don't believe any of them, the implications are the same: What you're doing right here, right now is infinitely important.

The one most important thing we should be doing is the same regardless of which scenario, if any, you choose to believe in. The meaning of life is to fulfill your potential. So all you need to be worried about is the fact that if you don't know how to fulfill your potential then the most important (thus, the only important) thing you can do with your life is try to find out how.

In order to achieve your body's physical potential you have to live a healthy lifestyle. How to accomplish that is well documented and understood. So explaining it here would be redundant. Our mental potential isn't so well understood though.

FINDING THE TOP OF A SPHERE

There are many contradicting theories about what the highest potential of the human mind is. Every religion, government, parent, culture, and subculture has a different definition of the ideal human. Some of these theories are very articulate and some are very vague. Some people even claim it can't be known. So which theory, if any, is right?

First of all, the idea that our potential can't be known is impractical, if not completely wrong. The fact of the matter is you're alive, and there are consequences to your actions. Those consequences may echo into the afterlife or they may just affect you in the present. Either way, they're real. Therefore you need to come to some kind of conclusion about what you should do with your life. If you don't then you cede control of your growth. If you let that happen there can only be two possible results. Either your mind will stagnate or you'll subconsciously allow someone else to take control of the direction of your growth. Either way you won't fulfill your potential, or you'll suffer a sub-par life until (and possibly after) you die.

On a side note, if you decide to take control of your growth and try to determine what your mind's highest potential is you should only accept those conclusions which are logical. You can believe anyone or any system of belief as long as their conclusions are logical, but you shouldn't believe anybody who tells you anything illogical no matter what authority they claim to speak by. In math the only authority that proves an equation is true is logic. The same is true for beliefs. Passing the test of logic is the only authority that gives words truth.

For this reason, from now on when talking about humanity's highest mental potential this book will prefer to use the same term professional psychologists use: "self-actualization." This term is preferable to "spiritual maturity," "enlightenment" or "growing up" because psychology is a science. It's not always an exact science, but it does seek to discover truth through reasoning and experiment. It should have no concern for religious or cultural dogma. Using the social-science term "self-actualization" reiterates the need to discover truth by analyzing your world logically and objectively.

WHAT DO ATHENS AND VIENNA HAVE IN COMMON?

The two questions we need to ask now are: What is self-actualization, and how does one achieve it?

The official definition of "self-actualization" is: "to develop or achieve one's potential." Oddly, that definition is vague to the point of being useless. It neither addresses what our potential is or how to achieve it.

Why was this word invented but only half defined? There's actually a fascinating answer to that question which cuts to the heart of philosophy, psychology, and the struggle to reconcile the interdependent yet often conflicting nature of the two fields.

The ultimate goal of philosophy is to discover truth. But what use is truth? It's only use to you is to apply it to your life. So really, the goal of philosophy is to discover truth that will help you in your life. But truth is ultimately of no use to you if you don't know what you should truly do with your life. So the real goal of philosophy is to discover what you should truly do with your life and then discover the truths that will best help you accomplish that goal. But what is your life? Your life is defined by what your mind experiences. This means the goal of philosophy is to discover what you should truly do with your mind and then discover the truths that will help you accomplish that goal.

In order to understand what to do with your mind you have to understand your mind in the first place. To do that you need to study your mind. The study of the mind is called psychology. So the goal of philosophy and psychology are ultimately one and the same. Philosophy just approaches the goal from the outside in, and psychology approaches the goal from the inside out.

Unfortunately, philosophy hasn't done as much as it should to help us understand life because professional philosophy has very few rules, and whatever rules it does have can be effortlessly broken with little risk of negative professional consequences. Traditionally, philosophers have just been random (usually upper class) people with a lot of free time asking random "deep" questions and stating their conclusions as facts. As a result it's not surprising that philosophers are rarely taken seriously. They methodology and thus their conclusions are too willy-nilly.

Professional psychologists, on the other hand, are (now) bound by strict moral and procedural guidelines. This sets a standard of quality for research and prevents unethical treatment of humans. However, it also acts like a straightjacket in the progress of psychological research or treatment.

Psychological research is by nature quantitative. If your experiment can't be measured and those measurements can't be reproduced with consistent results they won't be published. Thus they won't be accepted. This limits psychology because you can't empirically prove what the highest potential of a human mind is. If you make any kind of claim it'll rightfully be labeled philosophy at best or opinion at worst.

This means professional psychology has cut off its own feet. If you can't or won't decide what a human's highest potential is, then what's the end goal you're working towards when administering psychological treatment? Sure, you can alleviate mental suffering, but you can't go any further. So all you can really do is fill in the valleys and maintain the status quo.

Psychology doesn't have to be anchorless though. If nothing else, its goal should be to develop people's minds to the point that they're intelligent enough to choose their own definition of self-actualization and possess the skills necessary to achieve that goal.

The only way to take psychology to the next level is to know the meaning of life, because once you've deduced the meaning of life you can measure which psychological approach best facilitates accomplishing that goal. As long as the logic behind your philosophy on life is reasonable then your brand of psychological treatment should be reasonably credible as well.

This book argues that the meaning of life is to become you to the fullest extent possible. So the definition of self-actualization used from this point forward will be, "achieving the level of mental development where one has masterfully defined and created one's own identity and is capable of exercising free will."

There are five broad steps to achieving that goal. They can be summarized as survival, learning, thinking, defining yourself, and obeying a logical system of morals.

THE FIVE STEP PROGRAM

Here's a quick introduction to each of the five steps to achieving self-actualization. After touching on each of them they'll be explained in depth in their own chapter.

The first step is survival. If you're dead you can't do anything with your life. That goes without saying, but it's often overlooked that there's a skill to staying alive that can be taught, learned and mastered. It's called responsibility. If you don't have that skill you need to hurry up and learn it, because the only thing keeping you alive right now is luck.

The second step is learning. Knowledge makes up the building blocks of your mind. Every thought you think can be broken down into bits of knowledge. So everything you can think and everything you can do is determined by how much knowledge you possess. Thus, your success in life is dependent on learning.

The third step is thinking. Knowledge in and of itself is just inert data. If you don't master how to make sense of that data and apply it to life then the only good it'll do you is to regurgitate it to someone who'll pay you...like a game show host. In real life you need to think, because the better you can make decisions the better you can live. The less able you are to make decisions the less able you are to control your life or be successful at anything.

The fourth step is to develop your own philosophy on life. If you don't figure out life for yourself then you have no free will. If you have no free will you can't truly own your personality. If you don't own your personality then you can never be a true individual.

The fifth step is to create yourself. You have an amazing brain capable of memorizing entire books and devising ways of building space ships, and while those goals have their place that's not why you're here. You're here to be you right now regardless of how many spaceships you have. If you do create a bunch of spaceships and they're all destroyed your life won't be rendered meaningless, because the meaning of life isn't to accomplish any external goal. It's to create yourself.

As the universe incarnate you finally have the opportunity to experience sentience. And the whole point of being sentient is to be an individual with your own mind and your own wants, goals, dislikes, fears, that you choose or create. But if you don't consciously and systematically create yourself then you risk wasting millennia of hard work only to become a dull shadow of the being you were meant to be.

As a child of God you were created to become free-willed, fully sentient being. The point of creating you in the form and place you're in is to give you the chance to create yourself how you want to be instead of God creating you as a clone, slave or toy. But this doesn't just happen on its own. You have to take control of the process.

CHAPTER 11
SURVIVAL

"Give a man a fish and you feed him for a day. Teach a man to fish and you feed him for a lifetime." ~Chinese Proverb

"Life's tough. Life's tougher when you're stupid." ~John Wayne

Survival is the first step to self-actualization for one simple reason. You can't do anything if you're dead. Of course, we're all going to die someday, but this doesn't mean we'll never achieve self-actualization. It just means we have a limited amount of time to do it in.

This raises the question though, what about people, specifically children, who are bedridden with a terminal illness? Are their lives meaningless because they won't be able to fulfill all of their wildest dreams? No. Their potential is more limited than everyone else's, but they still have potential nonetheless. In fact, their potential should be even simpler to fulfill. That might sound cold, and on one hand it is, but that's only because death is cold and unconcerned with the hearts of man, but there's also a message of hope there.

Regardless of your situation in life you have potential. Your life always has meaning, and you can live a productive life even if it's spent in a hospital bed -even if all you can do is smile at a loved one. When the clock is ticking down you can waste your precious remaining moments pleading for mercy or cursing the sky or you can do the math, decide what the most important thing you can be doing is and then focus on fulfilling that potential.

A BLANK SURVIVAL GUIDE

In the meantime, there's a term that describes the skill of staying alive. It's called "responsibility." Everyone has heard this term before, but few people have a systematic understanding of it.

Have your parents given you a book that systematically explains how to be responsible? If they haven't then ask them when they're planning on doing that.

Chances are your parents didn't give you a book on responsibility because they never completely articulated that skill set to themselves. At best they had some good pointers, but good pointers aren't enough to help you put together a complicated piece of furniture much less live a successful life. What's really needed in both cases is systematic instruction.

Responsibility requires motivation, selfishness, knowledge of your environment, and the ability to make accurate cost or benefit analysis.

THE PRICE OF PRIORITIES

Any action your body performs, especially any system of actions, only happens as a result of thoughts processed in your brain. You won't perform any action unless you're motivated to by the thoughts in your brain. At any given time you're motivated to perform thousands of different, often conflicting actions. You can arrange these prerogatives in a hierarchy according to motivation. Which thoughts you act upon depend on which are at the top of the hierarchy at any given moment. In other words, you do what's most important to you at any given moment.

If you don't know why you should survive or if your reason is vague then you're not going to be motivated to work very hard at surviving. In that case you're going to work harder at something else. For example, if you tell your children they're stupid and worthless when they misbehave they're going to learn they're stupid and worthless. Then what motivation are they going to have to work hard at surviving? Very little, if any. In fact, having a low sense of self-worth coupled with the desire to eliminate the pain associated with a low self-esteem is more likely to motivate them to live recklessly and abuse their bodies. So this method of parenting actually teaches children to be irresponsible.

Here are a few possible reasons why life is valuable and thus why you should survive: It took trillions of years to create you. Relative to the age and size of the universe you're infinitely rare and thus infinitely valuable. You were created for a specific and special purpose. God loves you.

Regardless of what your parents or anybody else tells you, you need to come to your own conclusions to the questions: Why does your life have value and why should you survive? How many people really spend time thinking about that and exploring it, making it intimate to them like a favorite song? Very few. As a result, even though most people technically have an idea how valuable they are, for all practical purposes they have no idea. In order to make sure you understand your value on a meaningful level you should spend a good deal of time meditating on the topic yourself.

Whatever conclusions you come to, you should take this piece of advice: your worth is intrinsic. It's not related to anything that happens outside of your body. Your value is the same regardless of whether anybody loves you. It's the same regardless of any goals you fail or succeed at. It's the same regardless of how much money, power, or prestige you have. You're always infinitely valuable.

The effort you put in to surviving and thriving is directly proportional to how much you value your life. If you're 100% motivated to survive you'll figure out your own instructions and be able to solve any problem that gets in your way without any help. But just imagine how much more productive you'd be if you did have help. So here are some more instructions.

THE VIRTUE OF SELFISHNESS

It's easy to tell yourself in an abstract and philosophical way that you value yourself and are motivated to stay alive. It's not so simple to apply that motivation in real life. Doing that productively requires an accurate understanding of selfishness.

Selfishness is almost always frowned upon for good reason. Between ignorance and selfishness you can probably explain every crime and atrocity in history. So it would seem counterintuitive that selfishness can be a virtue. However, this perception is wrong. Selfishness is a necessary virtue as long as it's taken in moderation.

Selfishness is defined:

1. Devoted to or caring only for oneself; concerned primarily with one's own interests, benefits, welfare, etc., regardless of others.

2. Characterized by or manifesting concern or care only for oneself

It's easy to imagine how that kind of attitude could be dangerous, but what if you're never concerned for yourself? Or more commonly, what if you've never articulated your concern for yourself? That could be equally dangerous. What if the definition of "selfish" read like this?

1. Devoted to or caring for oneself; concerned with one's own interests, benefits, welfare.....

2. Characterized by or manifesting concern or care for oneself

You'd be hard pressed to find a better definition of responsibility than that. Think about any action you consider responsible: graduating school, obeying the law, paying your bills on time, saving money, avoiding debt, driving defensively, taking care of your body, etc. What makes those concepts responsible? Are they responsible simply because you were told they are? No. They're responsible because they benefit you.

The best example of this is smoking. It's irresponsible to smoke because it will kill you. So why is it responsible not to smoke? Because it benefits you more in the long run. It's the more selfish of the two options.

When guardians tell their children they should graduate school and not smoke, drink, or do drugs a lot of times the only explanation they give as to why is "Because I said so." Or "Because it's responsible." But that doesn't tell the child why it benefits them to follow that advice. So they have no motivation to follow those rules.

As a result the same scenario is played out countless times every generation. Parents tell their children how to be responsible but don't explain why. Then the children don't know why they should behave responsibly. However, they clearly see the benefit of giving into immediate gratification. So that's what they do, and after years of living this way they finally have to face the consequences of not preparing for the future. Then they finally start asking themselves, "What will benefit me the most?" Then they start looking at their decisions through responsibly selfish eyes and their lives make a turn for the better. After that happens the children go back to their parents, apologize for not listening, and admit that they should have followed their advice all along. Then the parents gloat and say "I told you so." But in reality for all practical purposes the parents didn't really tell their children anything. So the parents shouldn't be gloating. They should feel ashamed for nearly killing their children and making them waste half their lives learning one of life's most important lessons the hard way.

If guardians would give their children as in depth an explanation as possible as to why the rules they deem responsible will benefit the child more than disobeying the rules then their children would be motivated by selfishness to do the right thing for the right reason.

Parents aside, anytime you make a decision you should analyze your decision enough to determine whether the course of action you want to take will really benefit you the most. You need to decide what's the most intelligently selfish thing you can do for yourself in the long run.

We'll get into the issue of what you should do when your selfish desires are at odds with another person's selfish desires in chapter twenty.

LEARNING THE ROPES

Even if you understand how valuable you are and base your decisions on what will benefit you the most you still won't be able to make responsible decisions if you're ignorant of your environment.

Survival requires avoiding danger and obtaining resources: food, clothing, shelter, medical care, etc. All of these things need to be done in the immediate present, and their availability needs to be secured in the future.

How you accomplish this depends on what kind of environment you live in. A caveman would need to learn a completely different set of survival skills than someone living in a modern day city. A caveman couldn't survive in a modern city, and your typical modern day city slicker couldn't survive in the wilderness.

Because survival skills depend on your unique environment it would be impossible to write a book on responsibility that anyone, anywhere, at anytime could use. Therefore, one of the most fundamental skills to being responsible is being dedicated to analyzing and understanding your environment.

Any soldier, police officer, motorcyclist, or retiree can attest to that. Situational awareness is the most fundamental determining factor in surviving in a dangerous environment. And well, you're going to die someday; that makes life a dangerous environment.

Retirees are included in that list because if you live in a country that uses money then you live in an economic environment, and obtaining and securing resources is accomplished almost completely through obtaining and securing money. So the more you learn about making or saving or investing or spending money the more likely it is that you'll be able to have food, clothing, shelter, medical care, etc. today and after you retire. The less you know about making or saving or investing or spending money the less likely it'll be that you'll be able to have food, clothing, shelter, medical care, etc. today and after you retire. Unfortunately too many people learn that lesson after it's too late.

Have your parents given you any books about making money? If not, ask them when they plan to prepare you for life. Did or does your school teach twelve years of personal finance classes? If not, ask your politicians when they plan on making that basic, essential knowledge required learning.

Since there are so many accurate books already written about financial responsibility it would be redundant to go into that topic in depth here. However, here are a few quick pieces of advice for anyone living in a modern, capitalist economy.

- Financial stability will make you happier than luxury.
- Study finances.
- Don't watch television commercials.
- Have a financial plan.
- Start saving as young as possible.
- Don't buy an expensive vehicle.
- Be wary about investing in any investment vehicle that punishes you for taking out your own money before the system says you can.
- Don't buy (or more accurately, rent) life insurance. Save that money and invest it.
- Request to have your body donated to medical science after you die.
- Request either to not have a funeral service or wake or at least to have one as inexpensive as possible.
- If you must get married, don't buy an expensive wedding ring or have an expensive wedding or honeymoon. You might grumble that a wedding should be romantic and the only way to make it romantic is to spend as much money as possible, but the leading cause of divorce is money problems. Starting off your marriage in debt is the most unromantic thing you can do for your marriage.
- Don't have children until you're financially stable.
- Unless your primary job is to analyze the stock market or you're intimately familiar with a business you want to invest in don't invest in the stock market. You'll lose your money.
- If you do decide to invest in the stock market don't do it unless you have tens of thousands of Rands you can afford to lose. If you don't have tens of thousands of Rands you can afford to lose you shouldn't be risking your money in the stock market, and on the off chance you

do make money off the stock market you won't make much unless you invest tens of thousands of Rands.

• Buy a house. Don't rent. Don't buy a big house. Buy a small one and add onto it as you can afford to. Otherwise, buy a duplex, triplex, etc. Live in one unit and rent the rest out.

• There are people who own businesses and there are people who work for people who own businesses. The wealthiest people are those who own the businesses. You should create a business if at all possible.

• If you don't own a business you need a skill. If you don't have a skill you can settle for a college degree. Otherwise you're going to work a hard job for low pay for the rest of your life, and you probably won't be able to save enough money to sustain a secure retirement.

• You can plan for the short term without planning for the long term, but you can't plan for the long term without planning for the short term.

NOT EVERYONE IN THE NEWS DID SOMETHING GREAT

Even if you value your life, think selfishly, and understand your environment you still won't be able to make responsible decisions if you think illogically. In order to make the best decisions about your survival you need to be able to make accurate cost-benefit analyses.

You can find more proof of the benefit of making good cost-benefit analyses surfing the Internet; it's full of videos and stories of people making poor decisions. You can also see reckless drivers doing it every day on the highway. The end result of making poor cost-benefit analysis is always the same: suffering.

The concept of the cost-benefit analysis is simple yet profound. All it means is that when making a decision you should ask yourself if the potential gain outweighs the potential loss. If you stand to gain more than you stand to lose from the course of action you're considering then that course of action would be responsible. If you stand to lose more than you stand to gain from the course of action you're considering then that course of action would be irresponsible.

There have been instances in history where people have taken irresponsible gambles and won. However, there have been far more instances where people have lost such risky gambles. At any rate, on average, if you always make responsible decisions based on the cost-benefit analyses your life will consistently improve, and you'll experience the fewest setbacks...and your risk of premature death will be drastically lower.

THE PARADOX OF RESPONSIBILITY

If responsibility were only about survival then the most responsible course of action in life would be to work all day, every day for your entire life at the highest paying job you can find regardless of how much (or rather, how little) you enjoy it. At the same time you would have to save every penny you earn and never spend any money on any form of luxury whatsoever. Then, when you get too old to survive naturally, you would need to spend all your savings on healthcare to keep yourself alive as long as possible even if you're too sick and feeble to move or do anything meaningful or enjoyable. Euthanasia would be the worst thing you could possibly do regardless of how painful life may have become for you.

But what would be the point in living like that? Life is about more than just surviving. Working yourself to death is irresponsible. Working at a job that makes you hate life and yearn for death is irresponsible. In order to be truly responsible you have to balance the effort you put into surviving with the effort you put into fulfilling self-actualization. In some cases this may necessitate making sacrifices that will actually shorten your life span. But achieving self-actualization in a slightly shorter life will be more rewarding than living a long life in which you don't fulfill your potential. You might also find that the joy and peace you experience from fulfilling your potential will result in a longer life anyway.

In order to make the sacrifices that will maximize the quality of your life you need to become an expert at making cost-benefit analyses by weighing the cost of survival against the benefit of fulfilling the meaning of life. In order to make those decisions intelligently you need to learn as much as possible and master the skill of problem solving, which brings us to the next two chapters: learning and thinking. These are included in their own chapters because they're as necessary to achieve self-actualization as much as they are to ensure your survival.

CHAPTER 12

LEARNING

"Only the educated are free."~ Epictetus

"Education is our only salvation."~ George Clinto

"If knowledge can create problems, it is not through ignorance that we can solve them."~ Isaac Asimov

"Better to be unborn than untaught, for ignorance is the root of all misfortune."~ Aristotle

Ask your friends this question: Do you believe knowledge is important?

Pretty much everybody would answer, "Yes" to that question. In fact, the answer is so obvious the question is rhetorical. Right?

If that were the case then why are there are so many ignorant people in the world? Why doesn't every single person make it the number one priority in their lives to systematically learn as much knowledge as possible? Why do some people actually disdain knowledge? Why are there people who hate reading? Why are smart people labeled with derogatory names like, "dork," "nerd," or "geek?" Why are there people who discourage their children from attending college? Why are there even subcultures that think it's cool to be clueless?

It may seem obvious that knowledge is important, but it's also obvious that the masses don't understand how important knowledge is or why it's important. So even if they can vaguely admit its importance, since they don't truly understand its value they don't truly value it. Since they don't truly value it they don't seek it out, and in some cases they even fear it.

So in protest of ignorance here is the most important lesson you were never taught in school: Why knowledge is important.

Knowledge is important to a human for two reasons: internal growth and external action.

INTERNAL GROWTH

Look at your body in a mirror. It looks like one single object, but it can be broken down into organ systems, organs, tissue, cells, organelles, protein, DNA, atoms, protons, neutrons, electrons, hadrons, quarks, fermions, leptons, gluons, etc. Your body is a complex system that can be divided into ever smaller and more fundamental parts.

Your mind is the same way. Everything that makes up your mind: personality, thoughts, ideas, opinions, dreams, fears, desires, memories, skills, vocabulary, etc. are all made from different levels of progressively smaller building blocks. The most fundamental of these building blocks is knowledge. The more knowledge you have the more articulate and complete your personality, thoughts, ideas, opinions, dreams, fears, desires, memories, skills, vocabulary, etc. will be. The more mass your body has the bigger a person you'll be, and the more knowledge you have the bigger your mind will be. Thus, the bigger of a person you'll be.

This means that in order to grow up you need to learn. You can't just get old and all of a sudden claim you're grown up. If you stop systematically learning after graduation then it doesn't matter how many years you age, you all but stopped growing after you quit going to school. Therefore, you never grew up.

Imagine the personality of a baby. Aside from emotions and instinct a baby doesn't have a personality or identity. All those cute or sad faces are the product of instinct, not personality.

Now imagine a ten year old. The child has a personality but pretty much everything about his personality is still naïve. He has naïve thoughts, questions, beliefs, opinions, dreams, fears, etc. Honestly, you can't possibly spend a day with a ten year old without rolling your eyes at least once because of something naive he said or did.

Now imagine a regular grown man. He's a blue collar worker, has 2.5 children, practices religion but is no theologian, and manages his money responsibly enough that he doesn't starve. This man doesn't suffer too much mental distress and is capable of functioning in society.

However, he's never systematically tried to achieve self-actualization, and he doesn't go out of his way to learn new things every day.

He's really just on par with what a human is capable of becoming. His philosophy on life is basically to keep your head down, pay your taxes, celebrate holidays, watch television, and hopefully someday retire relatively comfortably.

This man will never truly understand the world around him. He'll believe what he was taught in school, and after he graduates he'll only learn what knowledge he stumbles upon, which will be mainly limited to what's on cable television. His thoughts will be limited to mainstream thoughts. His hopes and fears will be the same as his neighbors. He might not buy celebrity gossip magazines, but it won't be entirely uncommon for him to take part in conversations about it.

The life of the average man doesn't sound too horrible, but compare it to what his life could have been like.

Imagine anyone who has earned the title of one of the greatest minds in history. These people understood life deeper, made their own perceptive observations without waiting for other people to make sense of the world for them. They were empowered. They weren't slaves to mainstream thoughts. They had logical thoughts, rational fears, brilliant hopes, articulate opinions or beliefs and personalities you could lose yourself in. Their minds were veritable galaxies. They experienced life more deeply and rewardingly than the average man even has the capacity to imagine.

Whatever factors can be used to explain the differences between an infant, ten year old, adult, and genius there's one common denominator that's always present: knowledge.

Imagine if everybody's minds could be visually represented by the house they live in. A baby would be lying on a concrete slab. A child would live in a small slapdash shack. Your average person would live in a drab suburban cookie-cutter home. A genius would live in an elaborately customized mansion.

That's an easy enough analogy to understand, but it's easy to miss the depth of the message in it: that there are real internal rewards to gaining knowledge, and there are real internal consequences to being ignorant. This is who you're going to be for the rest of your life. This is how you're going to experience the rest of your life. By not learning you're condemning yourself to a dull and confusing mental prison. You're missing out on experiencing the fullness of life by not experiencing the fullness of yourself.

EXTERNAL ACTIONS

Every interaction you have with the external world: driving, raising a child, working at your job, making friends, managing your finances, cooking, voting, self-defense, teaching, putting furniture together, managing employees, finding a mate, living with your mate, etc. Everything you do is the result of thoughts you process in your brain, and those thoughts are made of bits of knowledge strung together. The more knowledge you possess the more articulate and complete your thoughts can be. The more complete your thoughts are the better you can do anything. The quality of everything you do, from the most insignificant to the most life changing action, is determined by how much knowledge you have.

Here's a real world example of this concept in action. The more you know about cars the better you can fix them. That's obvious enough, but there's a few things implied in that simple statement that a lot of people don't seem to understand.

The most basic implication of that statement is that you can learn about a car. It's possible just as it's possible to learn about anything. Is there anything you want to do but can't? If so, it's not because there's something inherently wrong with you that will always prevent you from doing that thing. You just need to learn it.

Think about this. Everyone wishes they had super powers. Why do we want superpowers? Because we want to be capable of doing more in life, and we feel limited by our feeble bodies. But it's not really our bodies that limit us. Compare yourself to a plant, and you'll see why this is true. A plant truly is stuck with the same abilities forever.

Most plants can't even move except to grow towards light. From a plant's perspective not only can we move freely, but we have the ability to choose whatever kinds of roots, stems, leaves, flowers, etc. we want. We can choose our defense mechanisms (martial arts, marksmanship), root system (investment strategy, job skills), flowers (art, music, fashion), etc. Compared to a plant you already have superpowers, but more importantly, you can choose whatever other superpowers you want. So if you feel stuck in life and wish you had superpowers then go learn something.

Think about how the car analogy applies to ignorance. If you can't fix your car you don't stand around wondering why. You know why. You can't fix it because you don't know how, but with a broken car you don't just sit around complaining about it. You accept the fact that it's broken and take steps to learn how to fix it or hire somebody who can.

The same concept is true with anything you do. Think about any problem you've ever had in your life. Think about any failure you've experienced, any dream unfulfilled, any mistake you regret. Think about any tear you've shed. Any time you've shook in frustration or anger. Have you ever sat around with your hands in your head wondering, "Why is this happening to me?" The next time that happens imagine yourself sitting behind the wheel of your car with your hands on your head feeling helpless and bewildered wondering, "Why doesn't my car work?" Because that's ultimately what you're doing.

Would you get upset and defensive if someone told you your car is broken or running poorly because you don't know how to fix it? Probably not, but everyday people refuse to take responsibility for their lives. They make excuses for the bad things happening to them by saying it's not their fault. They try to find anything to blame their problems on except their own ignorance.

On the most fundamental level ignorance is the root of all problems, and knowledge is the solution. If there's a problem in your life there's knowledge you can possess that will allow you to fix it or there's someone with the knowledge who can help you if you'd only try to find them. If you don't have that knowledge and aren't trying to find it then it's your fault there are problems in your life regardless of their original source.

Ignorance is even the root of all external problems too. If you were hurt by someone else it's because they were ignorant. Even what insurance companies call "acts of God" can be prevented with appropriate applications of knowledge. Houses can be built above flood plains. Trailer houses can be made tornado proof. We can erect tsunami barriers along coastland. Buildings can be made earthquake proof, etc. So if you're ever looking for someone or something to blame you would always be correct to blame ignorance. And if your life sucks then go learn something. And remember, if there's always more you can learn about cars then there's always more you can learn about anything. Life can always be easier.

The last thing that thing that needs to be said about fixing cars is that there's only three ways you can learn how to do it:
- It's forced upon you
- You stumble upon it
- You seek out

The same is true with all knowledge. People are forced to learn in school, but after graduating nobody forces them to learn anymore. That doesn't mean they'll never learn anything else though. They'll stumble on a little more information here and there through the rest of their life but it's not going to amount to anything truly empowering. And what's the opposite of empowerment? Enslavement.

Most people only seek out the knowledge they need in the immediate present (like how to program their new electronic device). People generally don't say to themselves, "There's knowledge out there that will make my life better, but I don't know what it is. So I'm just going to go learn as much as I can about everything until I find that knowledge that will make my life better." People don't do that. They just sit around and watch TV and assume they'll learn everything they need to know in life from sitcoms, cartoons, and commercials. But that's not going to happen, and nobody's going to cram the knowledge you need down your throat your entire life. And why should they? That's your job.

The fact is you won't stumble upon enough knowledge to empower you above the status quo if you don't seek it out on your own. So this is your warning or your wake up call. Seek out knowledge. Seek out as much as you can, but ask yourself what the most important knowledge you can learn is and seek that out most of all lest you waste your life acquiring relatively useless knowledge. And never stop seeking knowledge. Everything in your life (internal and external) depends on it.

CHAPTER 13
THINKING

"Most people would rather die than think; in fact, they do so."
~Bertrand Russell

"Too often we give our children answers to remember rather than problems to solve." ~Roger Lewin

"The important thing is not to stop questioning. Curiosity has its own reason for existing. One cannot help but be in awe when he contemplates the mysteries of eternity, of life, of the marvelous structure of reality."~ Albert Einstein

Ask your friends this question: Do you believe thinking is important?

Not as many people are ready to respond with an immediate and resounding "yes" to this question as they are to the question about whether knowledge is important. It's a travesty how many people don't have a problem with saying things like: "Don't think too hard." "Don't hurt yourself thinking." "Thinking can get you in trouble." or "You think too much."

The value of thinking is far less understood than the value of knowledge. In fact, most people can't even give you a good definition of the word "think" much less explain how to do it. So it's no surprise that most people don't make it a priority in their lives.

In order to understand why thinking is important it's necessary to first understand what thinking is.

WHAT IS THINKING?

What is thinking? Can that question even be answered? Thinking seems almost magical and unexplainable. It's not though. Everything that happens in this universe can be observed. Anything that can be observed can be measured, extrapolated, understood, and repeated. Even though you can't touch a thought it still happens in this universe and thus obeys the laws of nature. It can be observed, measured, extrapolated, understood and repeated.

Ultimately thinking is nothing more than asking questions or recalling answers. If you've ever had a problem you were trying to figure out and you sat there saying to yourself, "Think. Think. Think." but couldn't come up with anything it was because you weren't asking any questions. You were ultimately sitting there saying, "Ask a question. Ask a question. Ask a question." Or "I want an answer. I want an answer. I want an answer." But you never actually asked any questions. So you never got any answers.

How do you ask a question? Is there a system to it that can be learned? Yes. If all thoughts are questions and all questions are algebraic equations then all thoughts are also algebraic equations. Though instead of using numbers and letters for variables thoughts use ideas. Instead of using plus signs, minus signs, division signs, multiplications signs, etc. thoughts use the words, "if", "could", "would", "should", "can", "who", "what", "where", "when", "why", and "how." Instead of using an equal sign thoughts use a question mark.

All algebraic equations follow the same general steps to solve. Therefore, you can use these same steps to think systematically. Those steps will be explained in a few moments, but first we need to go back and cover why thinking is important.

WHY IS THINKING IMPORTANT?

Thinking is how you make sense of the data that comes into your brain through your senses. Once you've made sense of the data you can make decisions based on the answers you've come up with, and, just like with knowledge, these decisions affect our internal growth and our external actions. Between those two things thinking affects everything you'll ever experience.

INTERNAL GROWTH

The role thinking plays in your internal growth can best be summed up in a quote by Eric Butterworth, "You see things not as they are but as you are."

The world you experience is shaped by what you perceive and believe about the world. If you're a brilliant thinker you'll live in a brilliant and realistic world and you'll experience a brilliant and realistic life every moment of the day. If your thinking is over generalized, muddled, illogical, warped, etc. then you'll live in that kind of world and you'll be that kind of person. Even if you have every luxury and opportunity in the world handed to you on a silver platter, if your mind is illogical your life will be hell. Even if you have no luxury or opportunity, if your mind is logical you'll be happy.

EXTERNAL ACTIONS

As for external actions, every single decision you'll ever make in life is done by thinking whether you realize it or not. Many of these decisions are done almost subconsciously such as deciding to pick up a fork to eat your food with. Some are done semi-subconsciously, such as deciding when it's safe to cross a street. Some of them take a considerable amount of time and conscious thought such as deciding what you want to do for a living. Some decisions should be made consciously, but can be made subconsciously if you don't choose to think about them yourself. This is why advertisements can convince you to buy expensive things that logic would tell you not to. Any way you cut it though, there's some level of reasoning going on in your brain every time you make any decision, no matter how trivial or important.

The better you are at thinking the better you can make decisions. You'll drive better, understand people better, work more efficiently, buy less stuff you don't need, vote wisely, rule wisely, discipline your children accurately, be able to fix things around the house, etc. The better you are at solving problems the fewer problems you'll have in your life and the easier the problems you do have will be to overcome.

Thinking poorly has a negative effect on everything you will ever do every second of your entire life. How often do you make mistakes? Is your life a failure? Are you miserable? If so you either need to get medication or improve your ability to think, because whatever your problems are, there are only two ways to identify and or solve them: by thinking for yourself or by listening to someone else who is a better thinker than you...though, if you're a poor thinker you probably won't believe what an intelligent person tells you anyway. At any rate, most people can't financially afford to have someone else to think for them. So for most people it's either think or die.

Think of all the people you know. Who has the least amount of problems? Who seems to be able to overcome any hardship thrown their way? Who panics the least? Talk to that person in depth about how they deal with their problems. If you know several people like this then talk to all of them. Regardless of what ever other factors affect their behavior they all have one thing in common. They make a habit of thinking.

Out of all the people you know whose life is the biggest wreck? Who complains the most about their problems? Who is always saying the world is unfair? Ask that person or persons how they solve problems. If you know several of these people then talk to all of them. Regardless of whatever other factors affect their behavior they all have one thing in common. They don't think.

Another problem with not thinking is you leave yourself vulnerable to believe other people without questioning them. This means you surrender control of your life to another person, which is an absolute waste of your potential, because if you're not living your own life then your life is lived in vain.

What would your life be like if you never used your body? What would it be like if you could only barely control your body? What would your life be like if you allowed someone else to control your body? The results would be devastating, but it's a thousand times worse to never use your mind, have poor control over your mind, or let someone else decide what you should think. Next to learning, thinking is the most important thing you will ever do in your entire life.

THE BEST OF BOTH WORLDS

Here's another way to explain the value of thinking. Consider the graph below. A new born baby who possesses no knowledge and no reasoning skills would be all the way to the left of the spectrum while Leonardo Da Vinci would be at the other end. Mark where you believe you are on the spectrum.

Ignorance————————————————————————————

Now, without moving the mark you made, scratch out the words "ignorance" and "genius" and replace "ignorance" with "insanity" and "genius" with "sanity."

This accurately describes your mind.

The definition of "sane" is:

1. "The quality or condition of being sane; soundness of mind.

2. Soundness of judgment or reason."

People tend to take it for granted that most of us are born sane and only a few people fall off the path every now and then. But that's far from reality. To be sane is to possess sound judgment, to be reasonable, to be a logical and realistic thinker. We don't meet any of those criteria as infants. We can't, because we're born with a (more or less) blank mind. So technically, we're born insane. Think of a baby or a small child. If an adult acted like a five year old he'd be thrown in an asylum. Sure, kids have the excuse that their brains aren't completely developed and they simply haven't had time to learn life skills, but despite having valid excuses...they still fit the definition of insanity because they can't use the ability to reason to come to logical conclusions.

When tend to believe the only people who are insane are those who believe they're super heroes or talk to imaginary friends. And yes, those kinds of actions are insane, because they're illogical. But isn't it also illogical to spend all your money on lottery tickets, beat your children, bully your subordinates at work, act pompous, drive recklessly, insult your friends, buy ridiculously expensive jewelry, etc.? This is everyday insanity, and it's very real and very destructive.

Face it. We're all born insane, and going through puberty and learning the mainstream cultural standards in the place you happen to live doesn't result in full sanity. Just because you've met the status quo and can function in society don't make the assumption that conformity is synonymous with sanity or else you'll stop growing. In order to become fully sane you need to learn how to think and then make it an integral part of your everyday lifestyle.

A FORMULA FOR THINKING

We can all take control of our lives. All it requires is learning to think, for which there's a simple formula that anyone can learn:

1. Ask a question.
2. Gather data
A. Identify the variables you have.
B. Identify the variables you don't have.
3. Sort the data
A. Apply formulas.
B. Ask sub-questions.
4. Question your answer.
5. Apply the solution.

STEP 1: ASK A QUESTION

The first step in this process is deceptively simple. Anyone can ask a question; the skill lies in knowing which questions to ask, and, once you've picked a question, knowing how to ask it.

In your finite lifespan there are an infinite number of questions to ask and thus an infinite number of answers to learn. So which questions should you ask? You could try to answer as many of them as possible, but that would be futile. You could focus on trying to answer the hardest ones, but that would be foolish, because the hardest questions aren't always the most important.

You need to answer the most important questions first, and if you have time after that you can answer whatever questions you want. Otherwise you'll waste your life fretting over inconsequential issues while ignoring the questions that truly matter and have the biggest impact on your life and potentially every other living creature.

So whenever you ask a question you should also ask yourself if there's a more important question you could be asking instead. And at some point you should decide what the most important questions in life are. Then you should systematically answer them in descending order. Obviously, the most important question you can ever ask is, what is the meaning of life?

Once you find an important question to ask you need to make sure you're asking the right question to address the heart of the issue. Psychologists, doctors, and mechanics have to excel at looking past the symptoms of a problem and identifying or addressing the root causers. If you've ever been married you've probably had arguments that could have been resolved much quicker if you could or would have just addressed the real reason you were angry at each other.

Politicians face this problem every day as well. You can't eliminate crime by asking, "Should the death penalty be legal?" or "How many times should you be arrested before you're sent to jail for life?" Sure, those questions addresses crime, but they don't address the heart of the issue. So to focus on them is to hack away at the branches of the problem but never touch the trunk. To end crime you first need to ask, "What is crime?" Then you need to ask, "What causes people to commit crime?" Then you focus on that.

STEP 2: GATHER DATA

The second step of the problem solving process is to gather data (a.k.a. variables). This isn't just a good idea or something that'll help when you get stuck in a rut. You have to do it. If you don't articulate the data then you don't have any information to deduce the answer from. So you don't actually have an equation at all.

Intelligent investors know this well. They would never buy stock in a company without knowing as many variables about the company as possible. You wouldn't marry someone without knowing as much about them as possible. A jury wouldn't pass a verdict on a defendant without knowing as much about the case as possible. If you've ever bought a used car that turned out to be a lemon you definitely know the value of gathering variables before coming to a conclusion.

Sometimes we refuse to even try to find any variables or we refuse to acknowledge the variables that are right in front of us. This is why people say not to talk about religion or politics. It's common knowledge that people have already made up their minds on these topics and refuse to think about them. So discussing them (analyzing the variables) is futile.

Half heartedly identifying the variables in an equation can ultimately be just as bad as not identifying any of them. Just missing a piece of the puzzle can cause you to hit a dead end or make a wrong decision. This is easily exemplified in war. A general can know everything about military strategy, but if the enemy has one secret weapon or launches one surprise attack the tide of the war can change. Rocket scientists are no stranger to this fact either. When you send a space craft to another planet you have to calculate every equation perfectly or years of work and millions of Rands worth of research and design are going to end in disaster, which has actually happened.

The principle applies just as much with every day questions as it does with rocket science. If you're only half heartedly articulating the variables in the questions you ask then you're only half heartedly thinking, and that will get you half hearted answer, and that will either produce a wrong answer or no answer at all.

STEP 2A: GATHER THE DATA YOU HAVE

When you're solving an algebra problem in a text book you'll sometimes be given a few of the missing variables to plug into the equation. In real life you'll also usually be able to identify a few of the variables of a problem immediately, but inevitably you'll realize you're missing variables. If you weren't missing any variables there wouldn't be a question to ask. You would just see the answer.

To be successful at solving real world problem you need to be acutely aware of this fact, and after you ask a question the next thing you need to do is articulate the variables you have while keeping in mind that you probably don't know all of them.

Lawyers, auditors, and consultants all pay special attention to this step in the problem solving process. When they're faced with a new job they immediately try to gather all the information about the issue at hand. They know that they won't have anything to do if they don't gather all the data available. Then, only once that data is collected will they be able to find holes or areas of improvement on the data system they're working with.

What's the first thing a detective does after arriving at the scene of the crime? He analyzes the crime scene to gather any readily available data. When the murderer is standing over the victim with blood on his hands the detective doesn't have to think any further to solve the problem, but if the culprit has fled the scene the detective has a missing variable on his hands.

STEP 2B: GATHER THE DATA YOU DON'T HAVE

Sometimes you don't have all the data at hand though. In that case you have to try to gather the data you don't have.

Imagine you're cleaning your house, trying to put everything where it should be, and you see a dirty sock lying next to the hamper. No big deal. You know all the variables to the equation of "What should I do with this sock?" You practically unconsciously pick it up and put it in the hamper. But suppose you saw a gun lying next to the hamper. Then there would probably be some variables missing from the equation that you would need to identify before taking actions, such as "Is it loaded?" "How did it get there?" "Where is a safe place I can put this?"

What if, when you found the gun lying next to your hamper, you didn't try to identify the missing variables before taking action? What if you assumed you knew them? You might end up shooting yourself or someone else. You might leave it in a place that a child will find it. The burglar who dropped it might still be in the house. Never assume you already know everything.

Anyone who has ever worked in an office with an arrogant manager knows the consequences of answering questions without trying to identify the unseen variables.

Many businesses have been bankrupt by managers who assumed they knew everything and consequently made faulty decisions. Even in businesses that don't go bankrupt, an arrogant and ignorant boss can make life a living hell for the employees who have to cope with his poor decision making skills on a daily basis. Socrates would have made an excellent manager because he believed, "I know that I don't know." Or "I know that I know nothing." (Depending on the translation)

If you're humble and wise enough to try to identify the variables you're missing there are countless ways you can go about doing it. Detectives extrapolate clues from the variables they already have to point to the variables they don't have. Inexperienced small business owners who want their business to grow recruit marketing firms who already know the variables involved in increasing sales to tell them what variables they're missing. Students writing term papers just have to study their topic to death until they learn what they didn't know they needed to know. How successful you are at identifying the variables you don't know depends on how creatively and persistently you search for them.

Inevitably though, you'll have to make many decisions without knowing all the facts. That's life. All you can do is minimize the risk of making an incorrect decision by identifying as many variables as possible. Then, after the decision is made you should be mindful of your ignorance and be ready to jump back into the problem solving process if it becomes obvious you did in fact make the wrong decision because you didn't take enough variables into consideration. If you can't identify enough variables it might be wisest to abandon the whole situation all together. If you're a politician who wants to invade a country that you know very little about the wisest course of action is probably to just leave it alone.

STEP 3: SORT THE DATA

So you've asked a question and identified as many of the variables as possible. That information is only good for regurgitating until you make sense of the data. In algebra this means finding meaningful relationships between the variables. If somebody told you that A=B and B=C then you could easily see the relationship between A and C. They're the same. In the real world you also need to sort data by finding meaningful relationships between variables. But don't worry. It's not always that cryptic.

Suppose you just got promoted to assistant manager at your high school job. One of your new duties is to make the work schedule for all the employees. You've identified who works at the business, what shifts need to be filled, who has asked for days off, and who has any other conflicting schedules. Now all you need to do is to determine the relationships between each of the variables to determine who should work when.

Answering the question of who should work each shift should be easy if you have all the information at hand. However, sometimes the data set you're working with is much more complex than that. In those cases you need a more powerful tool to sort the data.

STEP 3A: APPLY FORMULAS

A formula is defined as:

1. "A statement, especially of an equation, of a fact, rule, principle, or other logical relation."

Every field of study has its own facts, rules, and principles for making sense out of data. The reason for this is because every data set has patterns whether you're talking about math, farming, psychology, interior design, engineering, biology, chemistry, dating, raising pets, cooking, fixing a computer, or anything else.

Without patterns data sets are just chaos. Very rarely in life do you ever find complete chaos. So anytime you're trying to solve a problem try to identify patterns and figure out rules to explain these patterns. If you're lucky somebody out there will have already identified the rules you're looking for.

If you want to find a mate there are patterns and rules for dating. "Rules of the Game" and "The Rules" are books about dating based on formulas (though their accuracy is debatable). There are definitely patterns and rules for making money. The book, "The Intelligent Investor" is one big formula. There are patterns and rules for making music. It's called music theory. Social skills are merely formulas for interacting with people. You might want to read "How to Win Friends and Influence People." There are even patterns and rules for everyday living. Collectively, they're called wisdom. Religions and self-help books are little more than formulas people have developed by analyzing the patterns in life.

There are also formulas for thinking. This whole chapter is a formula for thinking, but there are countless more sub-formulas. The more of those you can find or create the better of a thinker you'll be. Here are a few examples of formulas related specifically to solving problems:

• The simplest way to make the broadest changes in a system is to change the basics.

• If you don't know which direction to take when solving a problem then just shoot out in any direction, and eventually you"ll find a pattern to follow or a clue to point you in the right direction.

• Make as general and as vague of an answer as you can and then slowly get more and more specific. This way you can always reference your more specific answers against your vague ones to make sure they're in line with your overall goal.

• Consider the unlikely.

• The first step to finding the solution is finding where to look.

• Find a parallel or analogy of your problem. Seeing the problem in a different setting may give you a better perspective to see an answer.

• Consider the extremes. They'll help you put the problem in perspective.

• Ask if the problem you are trying to solve is one among many that stems from a more basic problem. If you can solve the basic problem then you can solve a slew of other problems in the process. Maybe the basic problem is one stem of an even more basic problem. Keep tracing back.

• A sign of higher-level thinking is being able to think in multiple dimensions.

• Another sign of higher-level thinking is being able to associate facts. A sign of still higher-level thinking is being able to associate facts from distant sources.

• A complex problem often has multiple causes, which would require multiple solutions.

• There are always at least three solutions to any problem, and if you can find three solutions you can find more.

Formulas are an indispensable way of making sense of mathematical and real world data. Undoubtedly you already use thousands of formulas in your life to identify patterns in real world data sets without even realizing it, but once you do you can consciously and systematically develop them. When you do you'll be a much more powerful thinker, and as a result you'll enjoy a much more successful life.

A word of warning though, many of the formulas people use to help them understand the world they live in and subsequently act upon are wrong. Surely you have a friend who is always asking, "Why do I keep dating bad people?" Your friend is probably using a bad formula for choosing partners. Countless people have lost fortunes in the stock market using faulty formulas. Wars are lost and governments crumble because of inaccurate formulas. So if you find that bad things are always happening to you it's probably not because you're the most unlucky person in the world. Realistically, it's probably because you're using bad formulas. You should humbly and brutally reevaluate your formulas.

STEP 3B: ASK SUBQUESTIONS

This step is where you're going to do the bulk of your actual work. The easiest way to explain it is to start with an illustration and go from there.

What's the answer to the problem, 12X34? Work out this problem on a sheet of paper, and you'll realize that in doing so you had to solve the equations 4X2, 4X1, 3X2, 3X1, 8+0, 6+4, and 3+1. You had to ask seven sub questions to answer the one question you really wanted to know.

When you think about it every step in an algebra problem is asking another question. The same is true with solving real world problems. If you're not asking more questions then you're not getting any closer to answering the first question. So if you can't get any further on a problem you're working on then you need to ask yourself, "What questions have I asked?" "What questions haven't I asked?" "What questions do I need to ask?" etc. You might realize that you haven't asked any questions at all, in which case it's no wonder you haven't found an answer.

If a detective is trying to solve the overall problem of "who done it" then the sub questions would be, "What is the motive? What evidence is at the scene of the crime? Who was the victim close too? etc." A computer technician will ask himself a series of sub questions when trying to figure out why a computer doesn't work. "Was there an error message? If so, what was it? Is the problem hardware or software related? Have any changes been made to the system lately? Is the computer turned on? etc." If your question is, "Which couch should I buy?" you might ask yourself sub questions like, "How much money do I have to spend on a couch? How much room do I have? What colors match the room I'm going to put it in? etc."

Each sub question can even have sub questions of its own. The better you can get at finding the right sub questions for the type of issue you're working with then the better you'll be at solving problems.

STEP 4: QUESTION YOUR ANSWERS

The next step in the problem solving process is to prove your answer (or anybody else's answer for that matter). If you get the wrong answer on a math test you might have to take the class over. Getting the wrong answers in life can cause misery, insanity, injustice, financial loss, war, etc.

A lot of times we don't want to prove our answer. We get the answer we want to hear and stick with it, but all this really does is create a fantasy world that keeps us from perceiving reality correctly, which causes us to answer more questions wrong because we're stuck calculating future questions using incorrect variables. This results in the illusion of a rosy world, but in reality it only propagates a dystopian society.

This is why it's important to be objective about your answers. If you're not objective about your answers then you're not a thinker, and all your answers are going to be wrong.

"Objective" is defined as:

1. "Uninfluenced by emotions or personal prejudices

2. Based on observable phenomena; presented factually"

On paper that sounds great. Nobody would say, "I prefer to base my decisions on emotional or personal prejudices rather than on observable facts." But everybody does it. People go to mind-bending lengths to conform observable facts to their emotional and personal prejudices even if it doesn't make any sense. Sometimes we do it loudly, and sometimes we do it quietly in the back of our minds.

Take this two question test.

• What do you believe strongest in?

• How often do you deliberately doubt and challenge the validity of that belief?

Ironically, the stronger we believe in something the less likely we are to question it. This type of stubborn faith is often praised as a virtue, but the less likely we are to question our beliefs the more likely we are not to take into account all the variables. The fewer variables we take into consideration the more likely we are to be wrong about it. So the stronger we believe in something the more likely we are to be wrong about it.

Furthermore, when you tell someone to have faith in something and that they shouldn't brutally analyze it you're really telling them it's good to be uninformed. You're being the enemy of truth. And for what? If we question an idea we're not going to hurt its feelings. It's not going to get back at us for cheating on it. All that can happen is we increase our knowledge and perceive truth more clearly. Whereas if we don't question our beliefs, all that can happen is we increase the likelihood that we're wrong. When that happens there's no end to the pain we can and will inflict on ourselves and others. There's also no end to how much control we can give other people over our lives.

How many people do you think have read this and said to themselves, "I'm not one those people. I wouldn't sell out truth for emotions or personal prejudices. I wouldn't think less about the things I believe the strongest." The people who say they won't sell out truth are the most likely to do it. If you truly believe you wouldn't then you won't guard yourself against it. On the other hand, if you admit to yourself that you have and will sell out logic for a selfish answer you'll be cautious not to let it happen again.

In fact, a wise person wants, yearns, begs to be proven wrong, because if you learn that you've been wrong about something then you can become right, and thus you'll have gained. If you refuse to be proven wrong then you might keep your pride, but at the end of the day you'll still be ignorant and will continue to make faulty decisions to the detriment of yourself and everyone else in your sphere of influence.

STEP 5: APPLY THE SOLUTION

On a math test when you solve a problem you simply write down the answer and wait to see if the teacher tells you that you got it right. In life applying the answer can be as easy as putting on the socks you've chosen to wear today or as complex as writing a book about the meaning of life. It can be as rewarding as choosing which foods you want at a buffet or as perilous as choosing whether or not to use lethal force against an attacker. The only advice there is to give for this step is to make sure your answer is correct before applying it. If you're unsure whether or not to act or you don't have the courage to act then you obviously don't understand the situation well enough. If you did there would be no debate left. There would only be action.

THE LIFESTYLE OF A THINKER

Learning how to think doesn't make you a thinker any more than knowing how to shoot makes you a soldier. Being a thinker is a lifestyle, and it's not a lifestyle that's only useful to a few people like the lifestyle of a soldier is only useful to a few people. It's not even just a skill that can be useful to everybody in the sense that say cooking is a skill that can be useful to everybody but you don't necessarily have to be good at it. Thinking is the way to be a successful, self-actualized person. It's vital for everybody to master.

Why do some people make a lifestyle out of thinking and some people don't? The answer isn't genetics. It's motivation. Either external circumstances forced them to come to a clearer understanding of life or they figured it out on their own. Either way, every thinker has come to some version of the same conclusion:

We're thrown into this life with no warning and no preparation. We're born lost. In fact, we're so lost most people never even realize they're lost, and nobody even tells us that. If anything, we're encouraged to just accept the world for what it is and to not ask questions.

To make things more confusing for us, the few explanations and instructions we are given differ from source to source. It's like trying to play a game you don't know the rules to and where everybody you ask tells you something different. The result is that we spend our lives bewildered and in a daze. And in the end all we have to look back on is chaos and anxiety.

But there's hope. If we can make sense of the world we won't be at the mercy of our environment. In fact, we can take control of our lives. How? We can perceive truth and empower ourselves using logic.

Being a thinker means realizing this and deliberately and consistently trying to make sense of the world you've been thrust into. It means the frustration of being lost and powerless fuels your curiosity to learn as much as you can. But this doesn't just mean reading as many books as possible and cataloging the information in your brain. It means constantly looking at the world around you and questioning it. A curious person wants to know how everything works, because the more you understand the more empowered you'll be. So thinking isn't a chore. It's a never ending opportunity to become more powerful.

The better you understand that the more you'll want to think. Thus, the more you will think. The more you think the smarter, stronger, and happier you'll be. The less you think the dumber, weaker, and sadder you'll be.

CHAPTER 14

YOU'RE SO LOST YOU DON'T KNOW YOU'RE LOST

"A child uneducated is a child lost." ~ John F. Kennedy

"You can understand and relate to most people better if you look at them – no matter how old or impressive they may be – as if they are children. For most of us never really grow up or mature all that much – we simply grow taller. O, to be sure, we laugh less and play less and wear uncomfortable disguises like adults, but beneath the costume is the child we always were, whose needs are simple, whose daily life is still best described by fairy tales." ~ Leo Rosten

"You are not responsible for the programming you picked up in childhood. However, as an adult you are one hundred percent responsible for fixing it."~ Ken Keys, Jr

Okay, so you've dedicated your life to learning and you've mastered the art of thinking. Now you need to put those skills to use building your philosophy on life. If the idea of writing a philosophy book of your own sounds intimidating, I have good news and I have bad news. The bad news is it's probably going to take a lot more work than you think because first you have to understand life. The good news is that it's possible, anyone can do it and this book is going to explain how. But in order to explain life we're going to need to take a step back and start from the beginning.

Consider how everyone's life begins. When you were born your mind was a blank a slate. Granted, you possessed some instincts and some aptitudes but zero knowledge and thus zero understanding of the world you'd been thrust into. Luckily for you, from the time you were in the womb your brain was soaking up everything you experienced and trying to make sense of it. It continued to do this the first several years of your life before you were even conscious of your own existence. Then, somewhere around the age of 4 you started retaining memories and became conscious of the fact that you existed. After that your brain kept soaking up knowledge, but by then you had control of the knowledge collecting machine that is your mind and body.

As an infant you hardly knew anything about the world around you. So you were naturally driven by awe and fear to learn everything you could about this mysterious place you found yourself in. You watched, touched, smelled, tasted, and listened to everything going on around you. You crawled into places you shouldn't have been to find out what was there. You opened everything you could. You broke things just to see how they would shatter. When you learned to talk you nagged your parents with questions that were profound to you but were so elementary they made your parents" eyes role. Your early life was defined by the quest for knowledge.

Throughout the rest of your childhood you continued to learn about the world from your experiences, your parents, your school, your friends, and whatever media you were exposed to. By the time you graduated school and moved out on your own you had a pretty firm belief system about how the world works. In fact, barring a traumatic event your philosophy on life was unlikely to change much after that. Unfortunately, this wasn't because your understanding of life was complete. It was because at some point the purity of your quest for knowledge was lost.

Somewhere down the road to enlightenment you started defending the answers you were given. Or you concluded you knew everything you needed to know and whatever you didn't know you made excuses as to why you couldn't, shouldn't or didn't need to know it. Or maybe you just became more interested in pursuing more shortsighted goals like getting laid, being cool, drinking, using drugs, falling in love, raising a family, getting promoted, being respected, or being entertained than understanding reality.

Many of the factors responsible for the stagnation of your understanding were present before you even became conscious of your existence. Your parental guardians were already imposing you their belief system or perception of reality (or lack thereof) onto you before you attained consciousness, and you were inclined to believe the messages they sent you without questioning them because humans are naturally inclined to trust the people they've learned to associate as authority figures. In time the philosophy they gave you was augmented or replaced by things you learned from your friends, school, mentors, and celebrities. While you undoubtedly learned a wealth of knowledge from these sources you have to take into consideration that in the same way your philosophy was influenced by the teachings of your elders, every person you learned from was also influenced by the teachings of their elders, who trusted their elders and so on and so forth back to primitive times...each generation more ignorant than the last.

Every civilization since the beginning of human history has had its own set of guidelines and rules for living. Even today there are thousands of cultures around the world with their own perception of reality...and they all (past and present) claim to be right, and since they believe they're right they discourage dissident thinking often to the point of killing people who don't conform.

If you'd been born 1000 years in the past or in the future...or if you'd been born 1000 miles away in any direction you'd subscribe to a different interpretation of reality. And from that perspective you'd believe with dead certainty that many of things you believe today are laughably absurd. You might even hate or want to kill people who believe the things you believe today. The point is that your cultural education was inherently subjective and shortsighted.

To make matters worse, the elders (and especially your peers) who pushed their explanations of reality onto you didn't have life entirely figured out themselves. You can test them on this. Ask everyone you know what the meaning of life is. Ask everyone you know to explain life in its entirety to you. Ask them to tell you their philosophy on life, and make them back up everything they say with logical and empirical proof. Do that and you'll find none of the people teaching you about life have it all figured out. In fact, you'll find most people only have the tiniest inkling of life figured out. Don't be surprised when you hear more excuses, logic stopping escape clauses, and resentment than answers when you put people on the spot.

Another thing you'll notice if you test people's knowledge is that there's a negative correlation between their certainty in their knowledge and the quantity of their knowledge. In other words, the people who are the most adamant and outspoken about their beliefs tend to understand life the least. This happens because the less you know the simpler the world is to you and the less loose ends there are to raise doubt. However, the more you know the more you'll realize how little you know and the more you'll be humbled by the discovery of your ignorance.

If you grow up learning from ignorant teachers you're going to learn incorrect information. That's a cut and dry fact. Now, this might not be such a difficult a problem to correct except that in your lifetime you'll have many different ignorant teachers pressuring you to accept beliefs that contradict previous ignorant teachers" instructions. In time you won't know what to believe. It's enough to make you throw your hands up in the air, give up, and not believe anything...or believe everything...or only believe the first thing you were told...or just believe what's most popular.

Again, this might not be such a difficult problem to correct except that even if you were able to figure out which teachers were right and dismiss all the wrong ones you'd still be faced with the problem that even the smartest ones don't have it all figured out. So their teachings will still only take you halfway to the shore of enlightenment, which means you'll still drown in the sea of ignorance.

The chances of you being able to fix any of these problems will be minimized even more by the fact that you were probably never encouraged to articulate your beliefs to yourself, and you can't fix a problem if you don't know what the variables are. Do you know what you believe? If so, how well? If you were asked to explain your philosophy on life right now in full detail could you do it?

That's actually a trick question, because if you could that means you've already written your philosophy on life down in blogs, essays, a manifesto, etc. If you haven't written your ideas down it means you've never worked them out. Could you calculate a quadratic equation in your head? Could you design every detail of a complex machine in your head? Could you write an entire book in full detail in your head? Unless you're a child prodigy savant the answer is, no. Nor could you get all of life figured out in your head. Solving a problem that huge has to be worked out on paper step by step. So if you haven't even written a one paragraph explanation of life, much less a book it's certain you only have an inkling of life figured out.

This raises the question, if you haven't gotten it all figured out yet and haven't written a unifying theory of life then how have you been making decisions all these years? It might surprise you, but even if you don't realize it you actually do have a philosophy you're living by, and if you don't know exactly what that philosophy is then you're not in control of your own life. The person or persons who slipped those ideas into your head when you weren't paying attention are controlling you, and that's a dangerous way to live.

If, when asked to present your philosophy on life, you responded by pointing to a religious book then you'd better be sitting in a monastery or religious center of some kind. If you're not then you're not really living strictly according to the teachings of your book. You're picking out the parts you agree with and making excuses to write off the parts that ask you to devote too much of your life to your religion so you can live the modern lifestyle you want. If you haven't devoted your whole life to your religion and yet you think you're living according to your book then you're only partially aware of the philosophy you're living according to, and that's a dangerous way to live. If you have devoted your life to your religion then you probably shouldn't be reading this book...unless you think God is bigger than your man-made, mythological religion and there's still room to ask questions.

Most people won't come out and admit they're ignorant and have no philosophy in life. People who claim to be religious won't admit that religion doesn't play a pivotal role in their lives either because most people just aren't worried about nailing down a coherent personal philosophy on the meaning of life because they don't think they need to. They believe they've naturally gravitated to exactly where they're supposed to be in life, which they use as proof that they're one of the smart ones who have life, if not completely, then sufficiently figured out. Yet if most people were asked to prove how smart they are by presenting the systematic, logical, empirically valid manifesto on life they wrote they'd immediately start making excuses for why they're excused from the assignment but still get an "A." It's human nature to defend yourself, but this instinct has prevented many intelligent people from waking up out of their sleepwalk and living a life worthy of the pride they take in themselves.

Consider the following points:

1. The vast majority of people are ignorant.

2. The vast majority of people don't think they're ignorant.

3. The vast majority of people are in denial about the fact that they're ignorant.

Most people would agree with these statements, but don't be so quick to laugh at the theoretical fools they mention. Ask yourself, how do you know you're not an ignorant person in denial? After all, the odds are stacked against you.

The test to determine if you're ignorant and in denial is surprisingly simple. On the scale below, where "0" represents the ignorance of a newborn baby and "10" represents someone who has life completely figured out, mark where you believe you are and where you believe the majority of other people are.

0——-1————-2————3————4——-5——-6——-7————8——-9-

Have you made you're marks? You're not allowed to change your answer after you've made it. Okay, let's see how you scored.

This test wasn't meant to determine how much you know, just how much you think you know. Regardless of where you marked yourself on the scale, you're ignorant. We're all ignorant. The only question is how in denial of that fact we are.

The higher the number you marked the more in denial you are. This accusation might offend you. You might be a very smart person, but if you're wise you'll put aside your pride and listen to the lesson the "denial graph" has to teach. The more complete you believe your mind is the less room you'll believe you have room to grow. More to the point, the less room you'll feel you need to grow.

Thus the less motivation you'll have to challenge your current ideas and learn more. Thus, you'll be less likely to do either of those things. So regardless of how smart you actually are now, your arrogance will slow you down so much in the long run that in the end you'll fail to fully wake up, which will cause you to fail to make the most of your life, which will cause you to fail to validate your existence. So all the knowledge you're so proud of today will have served no purpose other than to destroy you. However, the more you believe you're lost and ignorant (regardless of how much you actually know today) the more room you'll believe you have to grow, and thus the more motivation you'll have to challenge your current ideas and learn more. Thus, the more you'll wake up and validate your existence and that is the true measure of intelligence.

Now, somewhere out there someone is reading this thinking to himself or herself, "Ah, yes. I agree. People are ignorant, and none are more ignorant than those who think they know everything. I understand that because I'm wise and awake." But isn't that the kind of thing one of the idiots in denial who are beneath you would say?

"Oh, well, yeah." You reply. "I mean, I know they'd say that, but it's different when I say it because I'm different. I'm one of the smart, self-aware ones."

But wouldn't an idiot in denial keep denying their stupidity and keep asserting their superiority? Wouldn't an idiot keep saying, "Oh, well yeah, even if it seems coincidental the fact still remains that I'm smart. After all, I know I'm smart. I can prove it. Look at all the books I've read and questions I've pondered.

Your justifications may look good on paper, but you're still ignorant. Remember, we're all ignorant. So the more you maintain your righteousness the more you make a logical case that you're in denial of your ignorance. However, the moment you accept unconditionally that you're ignorant is the moment you take your first waking step on the path to enlightenment...as long as you don't start congratulating yourself again for how wise it was of you to admit your ignorance.

CHAPTER 15

CREATING YOUR PHILOSOPHY

"All truths are easy to understand once you've discovered them; the point is to discover them." Galileo Galilei

"The philosophy of one century is the common sense of the next." Henry Ward Beecher

Once you've admitted your ignorance your mind will be open and ready to start understanding life in fullness without being held back by ego or compromised by bias.

Now, a lot of people will tell you that life is an open ended question with no answer to figure out. If you pursue the challenge anyway don't be surprised when your own friends try to tell you to stop worrying about life and start living it. Also, don't be misled by their good intentions because there are some gaping holes in their logic.

First and foremost is that their assumptions aren't based on any evidence. You can't use the fact that you haven't figured something out as proof that it can't be figured out. At any rate, where would their advice really get you? If you don't figure out life then you won't know how to live it. That means you'll be destined to wander through life blindly hoping you make the most out of it on accident. That's what your friends are trying to encourage you to do, but the stakes are too high to take that chance. So the most logical course of action is to assume that we can come to some sort of conclusion about life and try to figure it out. Until you do that you can't truly live life.

The question now is, how do you figure out life? Think of life like a riddle. In order to solve a riddle you have to know the variables in the question. However, unlike the riddles you'll find in a book this one doesn't have the variables neatly spelled out for you in a neat little data set on a single page. You were born without any understanding of life, and the clues to solving the riddle are scattered across the universe.

So the first step to figuring out life is to learn the variables in the equation. In plain English this means you need to learn everything you can. Unfortunately, you don't have the time or brain capacity to learn everything there is to know. So you're going to need to prioritize what you learn, and in order to do that you're going to need to figure out how to tell the difference between important information and irrelevant distractions.

This means that the most important information you need to learn (at least in the beginning) is whatever knowledge will help you figure out what knowledge is most important. For starters this would include logic, study skills, and language (because the better you can articulate your thoughts the better you can develop them).

You should come to your own conclusions about what makes knowledge valuable, but this book will proceed with the postulation that knowledge is made important to you by its usefulness in helping you achieve a decided goal. For example, if you're lost in the wilderness the knowledge that will be most valuable to you will be that which relates to survival. If you're working in an office then the most important knowledge to you while at work would be that which relates to succeeding at your job. That much is obvious, but what knowledge becomes important after your survival is ensured? What do you need to learn after that? What is the goal of life after that?

That last question reveals the common denominator underlying the value of all knowledge. If you go around asking, "Why is this important?" "Why is that important?" "Why is anything important?" eventually you're going to boil the issue down to the root of it all. The goal you're supposed to be accomplishing with your life is by definition the meaning of life, and the value of everything you can learn or do is ultimately measured relative to its usefulness in helping you figure out and then fulfill the meaning of life. So you need to learn that knowledge which will most help you figure out and then fulfill the meaning of life. Yes, this book has already covered what the meaning of life is, but that's just one theory that someone else came up with. You need to solve the riddle yourself.

In order to narrow down what the meaning of life is you're going to have to ask yourself an array of questions aimed at cutting to the heart of the human experience. Even if, for whatever reason, you never conclude why we're here, or decide that the question is unanswerable you still need to come to some kind of conclusion about what we should be doing now that we're here. The following questions or observations should help you understand your place in the universe.

First of all, don't approach the meaning of life as if it were a "higher," mystical, subjective abstract topic. Look at it like a scientific problem and apply the scientific method. Or look at it like an algebra problem where you simply have to eliminate or reduce the variables and solve for the missing variable. This means your answer is going to be based on real-world observations and how you make sense of those observations.

Here are some of the questions you'll need to ask yourself in order to gather the data you need to figure out why we're here and what we should do now that we're here:

- What is life?
- How did life get here?
- What does life do? What use is that?
- What can't life do? What purpose does that rule out?
- If life didn't exist what would the consequences be? What would be lost?
- What are humans?
- How did humans get here?
- What can humans do? What use is that?
- What can't humans do? What purpose does that rule out?
- If humans didn't exist what would the consequences be? What would be lost?

Let me save you some time and explain a few common answers that don't pass the test of logic.

• The meaning of life is to reproduce. This theory is based on faulty, circular logic: If the purpose of every generation of living creatures is to reproduce there's no end goal. You're putting off a conclusion indefinitely. There's no point.

• The meaning of life is different for everybody. That's like saying every seed that falls from a plant falls for a different reason. Sure, they might go different places and grow into individual plants, but every seed serves the same basic purpose: to grow into a new plant. Likewise, every living thing was created by the same fundamental force and thus exists for the same fundamental reason. At any rate, the idea that the meaning of life is different for everyone is vague to the point of being useless. That provides no guidance other than to justify whatever mindless, selfish, preexisting whims people want to justify to themselves.

• The meaning of life is to figure out your own meaning. Prove it. You can't because this is another baseless theory that is vague to the point of being useless and is only used to justify whatever mindless, selfish preexisting whims people want and releases them of any responsibility for their thoughts or actions.

• Nobody can know the mind of God. For the sake of brevity we'll go ahead and assume without questioning that there is a God and we can't know the mind of God. That doesn't change anything. The reality of life is that you have problems you need to deal with right now to the best of your ability. In order to do that you can't let logic-stopping philosophies prevent you from thinking and acting.

Figuring out your own logical answers to the questions that will help you deduce the meaning of life isn't something you can just do in your head. The problem is too complex for that. So you'll need to work it out on paper to keep track of all the variables. Plus, writing it down will help you articulate everything you need to know. Also, it'll be easier to question your conclusions if you can see them on paper in front of you. Probably the most important reason to write your ideas down is so you can share them with other people. Imagine how much better the world would be if everyone throughout history had preserved their wisdom and passed it down to future generations to analyze, combine and refine.

ANCILLARY PHILOSOPHIES

Once you solve the most important question in life your next goal is to solve the second most important question in life. After that, the third, and so on and so forth. That means you need to figure out what the next most important questions are. In order to do that you're just going to have to use your problem solving skills and resources to figure that out.

Even after figuring out the hierarchy of problems in the world you're still going to encounter new ancillary problems every day because both the natural world and the world humans have created are limitlessly complex places. You'll need to identify or address many of these side issues in order to eliminate the problems preventing you from achieving your overall goals or to proactively build on your previous successes. This means you're going to have continue learning about the world around you and studying or analyzing the data with the aim of identifying the most important problems immediately in front of you.

As your understanding of the realities of your world increase you'll inherently develop philosophies which explain how things are, how they should be, and how to reconcile the discrepancies. Just like with your primary guiding philosophy about the meaning of life, you'll need to work these ancillary philosophies out on paper for all the same reasons. Eventually your philosophies should become so well articulated and organized that you could produce a quality book out of them. Having said that, it doesn't have to be the most profound and technically proficient analysis of esoteric PhD-level philosophical queries in academic history. In fact, that book probably wouldn't help you or the majority of humanity much anyway. Your book should sound more like advice from John Wayne than Sartre. The goal should be to make a book that is as salt-of-the-earth practical and useful to you as possible because if it's not useful then it's useless.

The question now is, where do you start creating your collection of philosophies? The answer is not to grab a cardigan sweater and a pipe and start making up bullshit. Take a breath and consider the question practically.

You were born lost, but as you grew up you instinctively adopted or created philosophies to make sense of the big scary world around you even if you didn't consciously seek them out or call yourself a philosopher for having figured out some aspect of life. Most of these philosophies you probably came up with after something affected your life you tried to make sense of it because it mattered.

So you've already got a head full of philosophies you're using to guide you through life, and most of those philosophies are based on the pertinent struggles in your life. Great. Write those down. Get a blank notebook and write, "I BELIEVE…" on the front cover. Then fill up the book.

Don't worry about filling up the whole book in one sitting. Express what you can. Take a break. Spend some time exploring your mind and asking yourself what you believe. Write down what else you come up with. Then go on about your life and watch yourself closely because you'll experience events that will require you to react according to your beliefs, and if you watch for it then you'll recognize and be able to articulate beliefs you've been living by but may have taken for granted and never noticed.

Keep a journal with you everywhere you go or at least keep one close by. If you can't take a journal with you be prepared to write down any insights you find on a piece of scratch paper and put it in your journal later. You should also make a digital backup of your work as well in case your journals are lost or destroyed.

At the same time as you're recording your existing beliefs you should also be questioning your beliefs to make sure they're logical. You should also be proactively studying the world around you and deducing new insights into life to write down. Don't stress out about making all of your insights fit into a neat, logical, systematic explanation of reality just yet. As you start really documenting life you'll just want to strike out in any direction and absorb or dissect whatever knowledge you can find. As you take this haphazard knowledge in and try to make sense of it your first insights into life are going to be haphazard as well. This is natural. So don't feel like you're not making progress when all you have are poorly articulated, seemingly useless disconnected bits of wisdom.

As you start filling up journals go back and reread your old ones. Try to find common denominators underlying each topic. Try to extrapolate each subject to find their extremes so you can see the whole spectrum of the issue. Ask yourself what you're missing. Eventually you should pick up a few trails to follow instead of only studying the world randomly. Once you've filled up enough notebooks and put enough of the pieces together you should be able to start compiling a systematic explanation of life.

Your overall analysis of life should eventually follow a pattern similar to this. Of course, you should question this pattern and see if you can't come up with a better one, but this is a useful place to start:

1. What do I believe? (This will be a general list.)
A. Why is each item on this list true?
B. What are the weaknesses in each theory?
2. What is the meaning of life?
A. Why is this true?
B. What are the weaknesses in this theory?
3. What is the best way to fulfill the meaning of life?
A. Why is this true?

B. What are the weaknesses in this theory?

4. Aside from fulfilling the meaning of life, what is the second most important thing in life?

A. Why is this true?

B. What are the weaknesses in this theory?

5. What is the best way to accomplish the second most important thing in life?

A. Why is this true?

B. What are the weaknesses in this theory?

*Continue asking what the next most important thing in life is as many times as necessary.

6. What is the biggest problem in my life that is hindering me from accomplishing my goals?

A. What is the cause of this problem?

B. What can I do about it?

7. What is the second biggest problem in my life that is hindering me from accomplishing my goals?

A. What is the cause of this problem?

B. What can I do about it?

*Continue asking what the next most important thing in life is as many times as necessary.

Anytime there is a hole in your philosophy where you haven't been able to figure that part out, insert a section where you devise a plan to figure out what you're missing. In the cases where you determine there's something important in life which simply can't be known you'll need to insert a section where you figure out the most logical way to live your life taking into consideration an unknown variable in the equation.

CHAPTER 16

MORALITY

"Never let your sense of morals get in the way of doing what's right."
~Isaac Asimov

"Truth is the secret of eloquence and of virtue, the basis of moral authority; it is the highest summit of art and life."~Henri-Frédéric Amiel

"What we call „morals" is simply blind obedience to words of command."~Havelock Ellis

"What is morality in any given time or place? It is what the majority then and there happen to like, and immorality is what they dislike."~Alfred North

An essential part of any philosophy of life is a solid moral code. If there's an afterlife and a God who'll judge your actions then it's of the upmost importance that you have as clear of an understanding of morality as possible because your actions in this life might be judged in the afterlife. However, there's an equally likely chance that there's not a God, a soul, a force that will judge your actions, or an afterlife. In either case, if the moral system you follow is incomplete or illogical then your life will follow suit. At the very least this means your life will be haphazard and unproductive, and it's almost certain that this will result in you being unable to fulfill the meaning of life. Plus, if you teach your children an illogical moral philosophy you'll set them up to suffer the same consequences. Not fulfilling the meaning of life is the worst fate a person can suffer regardless of whether or not there is an afterlife. This means you need to develop a logical and systematic understanding of morality, and you need to constantly reexamine and improve the system you follow.

DISCLAIMER

The purpose of what follows is not to tell you how you have to live, though you may decide you want to incorporate some of what you're about to read into your personal system of ethics. If you do choose to accept any of what follows you shouldn't do so on faith. Test the logic behind the ideas and make sure they pass. Regardless of whether or not you choose to accept any of the conclusions stated here you should still be able to use them as a tool to accomplish two things.

First, use it to help you understand that the traditional morals you were taught as a child aren't the final say on morals. You're allowed to dismiss them, analyze other ones, and even develop your own. You're not committing heresy if you do that. You're exercising the power of your mind as well as your free will.

Second, use it to help understand what a systematic moral code is and why it's important for your morals to be systematic. There need to be good reasons for every rule you follow, and there should be a unifying common denominator behind all of them. Any moral system should have an end goal. That way you can take any action and measure it against that goal to determine the value of that action.

Humans (have the potential to) progress through six stages of moral reasoning. Pay special attention to the last two words of the previous sentence, "moral reasoning." Morals aren't just answers to be remembered. Morals are a thought process, a formula to be calculated.

The first level of moral reasoning is most common in young children. They do what they're told by authority figures because if they don't they'll be punished. That's as far as their reasoning goes.

The second stage is basically defined by selfishness. Children at this stage believe that they should do what's best for them even at the expense of others. The only time they'll help someone else is if there's something in it for them.

The third stage develops in adolescence. Here the individual is primarily concerned with social approval. If everyone else is doing it then it's okay. In addition to basing morals on social standards people at this level of moral reasoning also tend to think that good intentions will justify deviant behavior.

In the fourth stage the individual believes the world has rules, and we have to follow those rules because those are the rules, and the rules are good because they keep us safe. This level of thinking is typical of older high school students.

The fifth stage is a little more abstract, and is easily spotted among college students. People at this level believe that laws are social contracts we make to keep us safe, but rights are more important than laws, and laws can be changed if we change them in a democratic way. People at this level of moral reasoning also say laws should do the greatest good for the greatest number.

If everything said in this book up to here is true then it's no surprise so few people reach level six. Most people don't learn, don't think, and don't try to grow. They confuse age and conformity with maturity. They see genius as different and thus as bad. They believe that since they aren't different then they must be good. So they end up celebrating their ignorance their entire lives. Thus, they never reach the highest level of moral reasoning. Is it any wonder there's no shortage of moral crimes for your local news program to report on?

So what's the secret to reaching the highest level of moral reasoning? Sure, you have to think logically and abstractly, but that statement is basically vague to the point of being useless. We can be more precise than that.

In order to think at level six you need a logical, systematic, empirically valid measuring stick. Each level of reasoning uses a different measuring stick: reward or punishment from authority, what you want, what pleases society, what the rules are, and what serves the common good.

The ultimate measuring stick is the meaning of life since the value of everything you do can be measured relative to how it helps or hurts you or others fulfill the meaning of life.

A LEVEL 5 MEASURING STICK

Let's use this measuring stick to develop a systematic method of moral rules. The system that follows is based on four principles:

1. A living creature's worth comes from the fact that it is alive. All living things are equal.

2. The meaning of life for every living thing is to fulfill its potential.

3. Every living thing needs to eat other living things to survive. Every living thing must vie for the same resources to survive.

4. The most basic need in life is survival. The second is safety. The third is self-actualization. The fourth is free will.

Let's take each of these four principles and look at them a little more in depth.

THE DOOR PRIZE OF LIFE

1. A living creature's worth comes from the fact that it is alive. All living things are equal.

Every living thing is infinitely valuable regardless, period. This also means that every person is equally valuable regardless of what they've done, what level of education they have, or what rank anyone has bestowed upon them.

One implication of this is that murder is inherently immoral as is the death penalty as long as the option exists to keep a murderer in prison. This rule also validates the Golden Rule, "Do unto others as you would have them do unto you." If everyone is equal then whatever you do to one person is morally equivalent to doing it to anyone else, including yourself. If you hurt someone else it's the same as hurting yourself. If you kill someone else it's the same as committing suicide.

FULFILLING THE MEANING OF LIFE

2. The meaning of life for every living thing is to fulfill its potential.

If the meaning of life for every living thing is to fulfill its potential, and everyone is equal then preventing or helping someone else fulfill the meaning of life is the same as preventing or helping yourself fulfill the meaning of life.

This means you're morally obligated to fulfill the meaning of life for yourself, and to the extent that you're obligated to do that you're equally obligated to help everyone else fulfill the meaning of life.

In this respect morality follows the same rules as responsibility outlined in chapter 9. An action is only responsible if it helps you accomplish the goal of surviving and fulfilling the meaning of life in the long run. An action is only moral if it helps other people accomplish the goal of surviving and fulfill the meaning of life in the long run.

Every society has rules that it considers moral that in reality have no relationship to morality. For example, cuss words have no effect on anything fulfilling the meaning of life. This means there's no logical justification for considering them immoral or punishing people who say cuss words on television or radio. The only basis for the supposed immorality of cuss words is cultural ignorance. The same thing goes for the taboos against masturbation, nudity, homosexuality, polygyny, etc.

SURVIVAL OF THE FITTEST

Every living thing needs to eat other living things to survive. Every living thing must vie for the same resources to survive.

The first two points in this system of ethics sound very tidy on paper, but they hit a snag when applied to the real world because every living thing needs to eat other living things to survive. Every living also needs to compete for the same resources to survive. Based on the first two moral principles this means we're acting immorally every time we take a bite of food or collect a paycheck. How can we ever in good conscience go on living knowing someone or something else has to die so we can live?

In order to get past this we need to take emotions out of the equation for a moment. The fact is this is the world we live in, and the survival of the fittest is one of the rules of the game. If every living thing is equal then it we all have equal right to consume each other in the fight to survive and grow. In cases where one living thing must die for another to live the one that should live is the one who is able.

Remember, this philosophy applies only to cases of life and death. Saying that the strong should survive is different than saying the strong should exploit the weak. Remember, we're all equally valuable. This means we're equally obligated to help those we can (when there's no immediate conflict for survival). Regardless of how strong you are it's still immoral to needlessly hurt or exploit those less powerful than you.

Look at how this applies to war and self defense. If it's wrong to kill then what do you do if a mugger or an army attacks you? Given that both your lives are equally valuable you would be justified in either defending yourself or allowing them to kill you. However, if you knew that your attacker was going to kill someone else after you then you would be obligated to try to kill them.

What about abortion? According to this concept abortion would be wrong if your only reason for getting one was avoiding responsibility. However, if having a baby threatened the mother's life or if food was so scarce in the local environment that someone else would have to starve in order to feed the baby then you would be justified in either having the baby or aborting it.

Let's apply this to stealing. Why is stealing inherently wrong? There has to be a more concrete reason than "because God said so" or "because it's against the law." Why would God or the lawmakers say it's wrong? It all comes down to resources. You traded your infinitely valuable life time to work for the money you have and the things you've bought with it. Stealing money or possession is the same as stealing life. However, this means there's no inherent immorality in stealing what has been stolen. Furthermore, you would be morally justified to steal if it were the only way for you to survive. However, that doesn't mean the law should let you steal either. The law has to protect people's rights. Of course, if we all managed and shared our resources wisely in the first place nobody would need to steal.

A LOGICAL HEIRARCHY OF PRIORITIES

4. The most basic need in life is survival. The second is safety. The third is self-actualization. The fourth is free will.

Life isn't just a never ending battle for life and death. Life is much more complex than that. Therefore, your moral measuring stick needs to be able to include every moral dilemma in life. In order to do that you need to have a well defined hierarchy of priorities. This doesn't have to include individual rules for every situation you ever encounter. That would be impossible. You simply need a list that is general enough to cover every possible situation, and that list should be as short as is practical to ensure it doesn't get muddled. Here's one such concise list:

1. The most basic need in life is survival.
2. The second is safety.
3. The third is self-actualization.
4. The fourth is free will.

When a conflict of interest exists between two living things the one who should be allowed to proceed with their interest is the one whose interest addresses the most basic need. When the conflict of interest is equal then the creature who should be allowed to proceed with their interest is the one that can. If there is ever a conflict of interest where it's possible for both beings to be reasonably accommodated without one trumping the other then they should take the path of accommodation.

CHAPTER 17
UNDERSTANDING YOUR PAST

"Those who cannot remember the past are condemned to repeat it."
~George Santayana
"Only by acceptance of the past, can you alter it." ~T. S. Eliot

Supposing that you've learned everything you need to learn about the universe you live in and you've mastered the art of thinking to the point that you can arrange all your knowledge in its appropriate place, you'll be left with a full understanding of the universe you exist in and a coherent, written, logical, systematic, empirically valid philosophy on life.

That alone will make you a successful computing machine capable of redesigning the universe to your will, but with no end goal established you'll only be capable of continually redesigning the universe to fit the ideal design which will allow you to continue to redesign the universe to the ideal state which allows you to redesign the universe into a state that allows you to continue to redesign the universe to....the same repetitive cycle.

You could spend your entire life striving towards this goal and leave it to every single one of your decedents, and you might be tempted to believe that all of your effort proves that your cause is worthy, but in the end, all of your work will only prove that all of your work was futile.

The ruler of the world dies just the same as the sewage factory employee. And when it's all said and done and you look back on your life the determining factor of how successful your life was isn't how much money or control you held, it's how self-actualized your personality was.

Unfortunately, for biological and social reasons, you didn't start consciously and systematically creating yourself from infancy. This means that if you want to start that process now you'll face a huge setback: the fact that the person you were raised to be isn't you, the person you were raised to be is a product of your environment.

At best this person was useful as a crutch to lean on until you were ready to stand on your own two mental feet. At worst the person you were raised to be is now an ignorant, insane, emotionally battered, schema-repeating, tradition-defending shadow of a fully grown adult.

Whatever the state your mind is in at the point you decide to take control of your growth you can't just throw away who you were raised to be and instantly become the person you choose to be. If you try you'll find that all you're really doing is putting on a mask, and you"ll constantly find the real you resurfacing.

In order to change the person you are you need to understand how you became that person. If you don't understand the forces that pushed and pulled you to where you are today you'll be powerless to keep them from pushing and pulling you back if you try to change. We've already gone over some of the external influences that are common to everybody, but every life is different. You need to understand your unique individual life experiences as well.

ASK A QUESTION

Use your problem solving skills to guide you in accomplishing this. The first step is to ask a question. "How did I get to be the person I am today?"

GATHER DATA YOU HAVE

The second step is to gather the data you have available. This means everything in your memory. The best way to start this process is by writing your autobiography. It doesn't matter how young you are. It doesn't matter how long the book is. It doesn't matter how eloquent it is. You don't have to publish it. You're just need it to be expressive enough to make sure you've articulated the formative events in your life. Writing your autobiography will also force you to articulate things about yourself and your life you may have never explored before. It'll help you make connections that were unclear before, and after you're done writing your autobiography you can use it as a reference for the rest of the process.

Even after writing your autobiography (or while you're in the process of it) you should tell your life story to as many people as you trust with that information, and you should also listen to or read as many other people's life stories as you can. In telling your story out loud you'll articulate more facts about yourself that you never considered before, and more connections will become clear to you. Listening to other people's stories will give you a frame of reference to compare your life to. By seeing how different other people's lives are you'll realize how varied life is, and it'll help you realize that a lot of the experiences you took for granted as inherent in everyone's life are really unique to yours. On the other hand, you might find you're not alone in your troubles. Either way, the more you understand how much better or worse life can be the better you can put your own life in perspective.

Another reason telling your life story is helpful is because if there's anything in your past that has caused you deep trauma you'll be able to reduce that secret pain each time you tell your story. It'll become more normal, more approachable, and more manageable. Eventually you might even get tired of talking about it. In which case you might even get tired of reminding yourself about it and reliving it.

As you write your autobiography each chapter should be broken into two sections. There should be one section for what happened in your external life: where you went, what you did, who was in your life, what they did, etc. Then there should be a section for what happened in your internal life for that time period. Ask yourself: How did the external events in your life affect you internally? What was most important to you? What did you think about the most? What did you believe? How did you feel? How did you grow?

GATHER DATA YOU DON'T HAVE

Now you need to move to the next step of the problem solving process and gather the data you don't have. This doesn't necessarily mean uncovering repressed memories. You might not have any, and at any rate, your memory isn't the only source of data on your life. The memories of the people who watched you grow up contain vital pieces of information about you.

Ask everyone you know to tell you about you. The longer they've known you and the closer they've been to you the better. The most important people in this process are your guardians. Ask them to tell you the things they never told you before. Ask your extended family to tell you what they never told you about your guardians. The better you can understand why your family is the way it is the better you'll understand why they treated you the way they did, and it might help to bring closure to issues stemming from how they treated you.

There's no one right way to gather data about your past. In fact, the only right way to do it is to gather as much data as possible. The only wrong way is to not gather enough. So get as creative as possible in learning about yourself. Remember, your mind is like a fine cut jewel. Each side of you has many intricate facets, and few people (if any) have seen every side. So the more vantage points you can see yourself from the more likely you'll see the whole picture.

USE FORMULAS

Once you've gathered as much information about yourself as possible you need to sort the data. This is where a professional therapist can speed up your progress exponentially, and if you can give that therapist your autobiography that will speed up their job all the more.

There are lots of formulas for identifying patterns in the human mind. In order to accurately sort the data about your past you either need to learn as much about psychology as possible or find someone who already understands it to help you. If it's impractical for you to hire a professional then you'll have to use common sense and acquire as many psychology books, journals, movies, documentaries, etc. as possible. Be aware of the fact that this level of introspection will inevitably have a huge emotional impact on you. The more support you have to deal with that emotional impacts the safer and more productive your journey will be.

Here's a few hints to help you get started understanding your past.

• Much of what happened to you in your past wasn't important. So you need to try to identify the most important factors in your development. Try to identify any events in your life that caused a change in your personality or belief structure. Identify any events that had a significant emotional impact on you. Try to understand why those events happened to you and how or why they affected you.

• Analyze the hell out of your guardians.

• If you had any traumatic events happen in your past they most certainly had a dramatic effect on you. Explore and express your thoughts and feelings surrounding that or those incidents.

• If you've behaved or felt abnormal your entire life you might have been born with an abnormal mental condition. If you suspect this is the case you should seek professional help to understand and possibly correct that condition. Though it should be noted that some abnormal mental conditions like high functioning autism aren't necessarily detrimental. So you might not need to correct the condition, but if you've been suffering distress because you've been taught it's not okay to be different and you can't change yourself it can bring closure to your distress and validate your way of life to learn that you have an abnormal mental condition.

• Identify patterns in your behavior and thoughts. We all have them, and if you've had them in the past and haven't identified them then you have them in the present and will have them in the future. These behavior and thought patterns will continue to control you until you understand what they are and why they're there. However, if you've been repeating these patterns most of your life you probably take them for granted. It might help you to identify your patterns by comparing the differences between yourself and other people or by having other people point them out to you.

ASK SUBQUESTIONS

The second phase of the data sorting process is to ask sub-questions. If you're not asking questions about your past then you're not making progress. The amount of answers you get is directly proportional to the amount of questions you ask. So ask as many questions as you can think of to help illuminate your past.

When you're doing this remember that you're not just making sense of individual events. No event in your life was an island. You're not just asking, "What happened to me, and how did I feel about it the next day."

Think back to the analogy made earlier about how becoming conscious of your life after infancy is like sleepwalking down a path and gradually waking up in mid step. The development of your mind followed the law of inertia. You continued walking down that same path until something impacted you with enough force to change your path of inertia. Then you continued down that path until another force acted upon you and pushed you down another path.

Everything that happened to you in your past was the effect of a cause. You need to systematically ask what the causes of your experiences were and what the after effects were. If you take the list of events in your life where your personality or belief structure changed you should be able to connect the series of events chronologically that changed you from who you were the first year of your waking life into the person you are today. You should be able to take any two years in your past at random and articulately explain how your identity at both ages were different. You should also be able to understand and list every step and factor that explains how your younger identity changed into your older identity. You won't be able to do that without asking questions.

Apply the same process to understand how your beliefs evolved. Also, know that all of your beliefs were learned either from external sources, created by you alone, or learned from external sources and modified by you. Identify where your beliefs came from, and try to remember if you learned the reasons for the belief after you accepted the belief. If that's ever the case you should strongly question that particular belief.

QUESTION YOUR ANSWERS

If you try to understand your past you'll probably come to a point where you feel comfortable that you've got it all figured out. That's the point where you stop growing and start taking fallacies for granted again. So keep questioning your answers. Your life depends on it.

APPLY THE SOLUTION

Every step of the problem solving process so far has really just been the first several steps of solving a much larger problem. All you've really done so far is gather data. If you've truly gathered all the data in the equation then the answers should fall into place easily. Spend as much time as you can going back over the data you've gathered and making sure you understand how everything is connected, and where all the arrows are pointing to. When you do you'll see yourself, the world around you, and the path before you clearly.

CHAPTER 18
UNDERSTANDING THE PRESENT

"What you need to know about the past is that no matter what has happened, it has all worked together to bring you to this very moment. And this is the moment you can choose to make everything new. Right now." ~ Afrizeet

"The past is our definition. We may strive, with good reason, to escape it, or to escape what is bad in it, but we will escape it only by adding something better to it."~ Wendell Berry

ASK A QUESTION

Once you've analyzed the past you need to analyze the present. In other words, you need to analyze who you are today. So ask yourself, "Who am I today?"

GATHER DATA YOU HAVE

Even if you've already written a gigantic autobiography you still need to write an essay that starts with the words, "I am..." Articulate who you are. If you've never done that then how well can you truly know yourself?

As you go through your day to day life, watch for patterns in your behavior. Once you've identified them try to figure out where in your past they started and how the existence of that pattern has affected your life.

Pay close attention to your thoughts. You'll find that on any given day you repeat the same thoughts over and over again. If you're having a bad day you'll constantly think negative thoughts. If you're in a hurry you'll constantly think about being rushed. If you're having a good day you'll think positive thoughts. But what kind of thoughts do you think on a normal day? What do you constantly reaffirm to yourself? You need to know that, because you are what you think.

GATHER DATA YOU DON'T HAVE

An objective tool to help shed light on what you don't know about yourself is a professional personality test like the Myers-Briggs personality inventory. It's expensive, but it can tell you a lot about yourself and can even help you realize that your personality quirks aren't bad things; they're a valid part of who you are. You can take free personality test online, but a professional one will help you a thousand times more. If there's anything in the world worth spending money on its improving your mind.

Hopefully you've already asked everyone to tell you about your past. Now you need to ask everyone you know to tell you about the present. They all know things about you that they aren't telling you, and you need that information. The first question you might want to ask is, "How do I suck?" You have a basket of personality flaws, and everyone's noticed them, but they don't want to tell you. They might have even told you but you didn't listen. People tend to do that and make excuses for their behavior. Now is the time to stop making excuses, admit your flaws, analyze them, and figure out how to correct them.

Probably the best way to learn about yourself is to move to a foreign country if at least for a little while. Everything you've ever taken for granted will be challenged, and you'll be introduced to a whole new way of viewing and living life. Your schemas will be shattered, and you'll be forced to reexamine your whole understanding of what it means to be human.

That exercise is impractical for most people, but without going that far you can still benefit (more than you can probably imagine) simply by going (alone) on a retreat to an isolated location far away from your home. Use your vacation time to stay at a monastery or a cheap hotel in the mountains or something along those lines. When we spend every day running in the same circles, seeing the same people we begin to take ourselves, the people around us, and life in general for granted. By separating yourself from everything you use to define yourself you'll be forced to face what's truly there, and what you find may shock you.

SORT THE DATA

Anything else you can think of to help measure who you are today will be invaluable to your growth in the future. As you gather that data sort it. Use psychology to understand it and ask sub questions to peer beneath the surface. Question everything.

As you do these things write down your results. It'll help you articulate who you are and what you believe. This'll benefit you in the immediate present, and it'll also give you a reference to go back to later. If you don't have that reference point on paper you'll surely forget it in time, and much of that progress will be lost. Remember, the dullest pencil has a better memory than the sharpest mind.

Having said that, not all of this process is a detective game, nor can it all be plotted on a piece of paper. A great deal of what you learn about yourself will be done by sitting alone and listening to your thoughts, focusing on what it feels like to be you, and becoming more familiar with yourself by paying attention to yourself. Basically, that means being more self-conscious. Self-consciousness is typically viewed as insecure and vain, which is one of the reasons why so many people have blank minds. They were led astray from the virtuous goal of paying attention to themselves.

One last piece of advice worth mentioning on sorting the data of your present is that you need to sort out the bad data. You are what you experience. Choosing to expose yourself to television commercials, idiotic sitcoms, or pop music is like pouring water into a sinking ship. You need to self-censor any garbage that might degrade your mind.

QUESTION YOUR ANSWERS

As you watch, study, and analyze yourself you'll begin to develop and later solidify your personality. As you do that you may become confident in your conclusions and content with who you've become. Be wary of this. It could either be a sign that you're nearing the end of your journey or it could be a sign that you've hit a dead end. When you think you've found all the answers start questioning them.

APPLY THE SOLUTION

Once you come to know who you are you need to keep watching yourself just as closely as you did before you crossed that line. When you know what thoughts and behavior you want or don't want to see in yourself you can become skilled at controlling yourself. As you use that skill you'll refine that skill. As you refine that skill you'll turn being you into an art form. It's like dancing, practicing martial arts, singing, painting, or playing an instrument with every thought you think, every movement you make, and every word you say, and it's projected into everything you see or hear.

You'll have fun no matter what you're doing because it's not about what you're doing. It's about who you are. Thus you'll be content. That means you'll be happy here and now without having to get a better job, friend, home, car, child, or whatever else we think we need before we can be happy. You'll effortlessly let go of the desires that keep you from attaining enlightenment simply by grasping to understand yourself.

Becoming you is like writing a good story. The key ingredient that every aspect of a story is hinged upon isn't plot. It's character. The plot is defined by the characters. The setting reflects the characters. The dialogue (which is the key to character progression) is definitely controlled by the characters. If the characters are perfect the story will naturally wrap itself around the characters perfectly. If the characters are poorly written then there's no way they'll fit into any story with balance. The quality of your story will only be as solid and enjoyable as the character you are, and you're the only person who can create your character.

CHAPTER 19

UNDERSTANDING YOUR FUTURE

"We should all be concerned about the future because we will have to spend the rest of our lives there."~ Charles F. Kettering

"We are made wise not by the recollection of our past, but by the responsibility for our future."~ George Bernard Shaw

Once you've achieved a practical understanding of who you are and how you became that person you're ready to reinvent yourself in your own image. You're ready to become the person you want to be. To do this you'll need to start the problem solving process over again.

ASK A QUESTION

The first step is to ask a question: "Who do I want to be?"

When answering this question there are a few things you need to take into consideration. The first is that there are almost no limitations. You don't have to worry about what your guardians want you to be. You don't have to worry about what society says you have to be. You don't have to worry about what anybody or anything says you have to be. The only authority anyone has over you (the only authority anyone has ever had over you) is the authority you give them. Once you know that you're completely free to become whatever you want; you're limited only by the depth of your dreams.

HOWEVER...

Heed these two warnings.

First, no matter who you choose to be, if you're ignorant then it's all for nothing. Your belief structure is the skeleton of your mind. If the skeletal structure of your mind is warped and broken then no matter how elegant the rest of your mind appears it'll still be warped and broken. The result is that you'll experience a warped and broken reality, your ability to grow will be severely limited, and your actions will be illogical, which will make you a danger to yourself and others.

There are three things you need to do to keep from being stupid. All of them have already mentioned, but this is important enough to mention again. The first two things are: You have to be committed to learning and thinking, and that applies to your entire lifespan. The third thing you need to do immediately after you understand your past and your present is to systematically deconstruct your entire belief structure, analyze everything logically, and toss out everything that's illogical. Put extra emphasis on the phrases, "deconstruct your entire belief structure" and "toss out everything that's illogical." So take the list you made of everything you believe and one by one write down why all of those beliefs are logical and illogical. Then question those beliefs.

The second warning is that choosing not to make a choice is the wrong choice. If you don't make that choice then everything you've done up to this point will have been for nothing. You'll go right back to allowing your identity to be defined by external forces, and then you'll never take ownership of your life, and your life will have been in vain.

In the same vein of reasoning, making an inarticulate choice is just as bad as not making any choice.

If you just say, "I want to be a better person." you haven't really chosen anything. If you say, "Okay, I want to be an astronaut." that's a little better, but there's more to life than picking what you want to do for a living. This brings us to the second step of the problem solving process.

GATHER THE DATA YOU HAVE

In order to become the person you want to be you have to pick who you want to be. This is easily confused with the question, "What do you want to be?" Forget about what you want to do for a living, and imagine yourself being locked in prison for the next twenty years. Inside that cell, who do you want to be? What do you want your mind to be like? What do you want your personality to be like? What personal strengths do you want to have?

Dig through your memories; have you ever seen someone on television or met someone at a party and thought to yourself, "I wish I could be like that." I wish I could be that funny. I wish I could be that positive. I wish I could be that insightful. I wish I could be that outgoing. I wish I could be that comfortable with solitude. I wish I could be that self-confident. What character traits do you envy or admire? You can own those traits. You just need to identify them and write them down so you can focus on developing them.

If you can remember ever admiring a person (real or fictional) then you can probably also remember making excuses to yourself as to why you'll never be as good as that person. Those excuses are a lie. Maybe somebody else gave you those self-defeating ideas. Maybe they're all your own. Either way, it's just a matter of who's telling you the lie.

The difference between any two humans is a practically insignificant fraction. It's been said in just about every self-help book that the determining factor in achieving greatness is almost always determination, not inborn genius. So success is merely a matter of motivation.

When you imagine who you want to be, don't tell yourself you can't become that because you're not able. Instead, ask yourself what motivation you're lacking that has kept you from becoming what you're truly capable of.

GATHER THE DATA YOU DON'T HAVE

Surely you can gather more data on the kind of person you want to be. So look for it, and as you're doing that keep in mind that the dreams that come true for you will only be as vibrant as you dream them, and one good thing about dreams is there are no plagiarism laws protecting them. Pay attention to everything around you. If you see someone you envy or admire then you've struck gold. You've identified what you want to become. Now become that. The only person who can stop you is you.

Don't just rely on identifying people you happen to come across. Get scientific about this. Find out what your favorite hero's personality type is and research that personality type to death. Study similar people. There's bound to be a historical figure who you admired. Study how that person achieved his or her goals. Your success in this goal is limited only by your tenacity and creativity.

There may be a hero out there who is perfect for you but whom you've never been introduced to, especially if you never leave your house or try new things. Get out into the world and study it systematically. Experience art. Experience literature. Experience other cultures. Experience everything life has to offer, and go through these adventures with the eye of a treasure hunter, always looking for new personality traits and skills to plunder and add to your intellectual wealth.

SORT THE DATA

Having an idea of who you want to be is useless unless you make (and execute) a realistic plan to bridge the gap between who you are and who you want to be. The process of doing that will be unique to every individual depending on your current strengths and weaknesses and the goals you want to reach. So it would be impossible to get too specific about how to do that, but if you know how to think then you should be able to create a productive plan yourself. Here's a few bits of advice though.

You're not starting this process from a blank slate. You already have a mind full of personality traits. So one of the first things you need to do is take a good long look at yourself as you are today and decide which existing character traits you want to keep and which you want to discard.

Reinventing yourself doesn't necessarily mean changing everything that makes you who you are. Likewise, keeping parts of your personality from your past doesn't necessarily mean you're living in someone's shadow...as long as you take ownership of those traits. Once you acknowledge that parts of your personality were created by your environment you can then choose to keep them. At that point they cease to be a part of you because they were thrust upon you, and they continue to be a part of you only because you choose to keep them. By making that choice you take ownership of those traits.

Tossing out the parts of yourself you don't want can't always be done with the flick of a thought though. It might take a significant amount of work to let go of the past. You need to figure out what it's going to take to make that happen. Then you need to make a plan to accomplish that goal. Then you need to execute that plan, but be warned that brute strength of will alone probably won't see you through the completion of your goal.

Take codependency for example. Suppose you realize you have codependent tendencies. Deciding not to be codependent and then fighting the urge when you recognize it might not work out too well. You need to ask yourself, "What are you fighting? Why are you fighting it?" If you don't know the answers to those questions then you're fighting a ghost. However, by trying to more fully understand your codependent tendencies (what they are, why they're there, and the consequences of that type of behavior) you'll make the decision to change more and more effortless. If you can see the situation crystal clear then there won't be contradicting feelings to fight. You'll simply see the way and there will be no choice. Quitting smoking is the same way. So if you want to change yourself then you need to work towards seeing the areas you want to improve as clearly as possible until all you see is the way forward.

Taking ownership of the aspects of your personality that you want to keep and throwing out what you don't probably won't completely bridge the gap between who you are and who you want to be...unless you're pretty much content with who you are. Otherwise you're going to have to do the leg work to create the traits you want that aren't currently there. This is going to take a lot of work, and more importantly, a lot of intelligence. You simply can't complete this phase of the process if you're ignorant, because your plan has to be realistic.

It doesn't matter how ridiculous or impossible your dreams are. You can accomplish them, but the cute cartoons from Saturday morning lied to you. Your dreams aren't going to come true just by believing in them. Your dreams are going to come true by understanding the real world obstacles between you and your dreams and then using logic and creative thinking to overcome or circumvent those obstacles.

Even if you die in pursuit of your dream before seeing it come to fruition...you'll have died in pursuit of your dream. And the time you spent alive will have had a meaningful personal purpose. That's more than a lot of people can say. You can't ask for much more than that in life.

QUESTION YOUR ANSWERS

You should live life with an articulate idea of who you want to become, and you should have a detailed plan of how to become that person. Yet as you spend the fleeting and irreplaceable moments of your life working towards that goal be ever mindful of whom you wanted to be when you were ten, fifteen, twenty, twenty five years old, etc. Chances are your dreams as a child were naïve. If history is any indicator of the future then in ten years you're going to look back at the journals you're writing today and laugh at how naïve they were. Don't wait until then to question your answers. Save yourself the time and do it now. Talk about your answers to people you respect. Let them question your answers for you. They can probably help steer you straight.

APPLY THE SOLUTION

Once you understand how your past molded you into the person you are today and you've gotten to know the person you are as intimately as possible the only thing left to do is to mold that person into who you want to be.

This is done partly by dreaming, partly by expressing yourself, partly by learning, partly by thinking, and partly by acting. This isn't a door you walk through. It's not a means to an end. Even though it's a path you walk, every step is an end to the means in and of itself.

CHAPTER 20

WHAT NEXT?

"A race of altruists is necessarily a race of slaves. A race of free men is necessarily a race of egoists"~ Max Stirner

"Until you make peace with who you are you will never be content with what you have."~ Doris Mortman

What do you do after you've achieved self-actualization? Well, that question is misleading, actually. Self-actualization is a door you walk through, but on the other side of the door is a path, one perfectly tailored for you. Once you achieve self-actualization you simply spend the rest of your life walking your own path.

Once you've found this path you'll know who you are. That will give you total control over yourself for the first time in your life. That will provide you with clear cut goals in life so you won't be wandering through life aimlessly. It'll eliminate the confusion inherent in an uncertain life, and you'll feel like your life has purpose, because it will have purpose.

Walking this path you'll know true happiness. Happiness is elusive if you think of it as this magical, transcendental experience. In reality happiness is simple. It's synonymous with contentment. To be content is to be satisfied with what you have.

If you don't know exactly what you want out of life then you'll never be content because you'll have never set the conditions for contentment. If you're never content you'll always be discontent. Well, if you don't truly know who you are then you'll never truly know what you want. So you'll never be able to attain what you want out of life and find contentment much less happiness.

The final reason you'll be able to achieve true happiness is because you'll know what's important in life and you'll focus on those things single-mindedly and abandon all the hollow ambitions you used to stress over so much. Until you've achieved self-actualization you'll leave yourself vulnerable to someone else setting the conditions for you, which will probably involve attaining an illogical and unrealistic level of wealth and social status which will definitely make you unhappy forever.

So what do you do after you achieve self-actualization? Live life to its fullest.

A FINAL WORD

My worst fear is that someone will read this book and believe every bit of it without thinking putting it to the test of truth and then mindlessly defend it or even go as far as to tell other people to believe it without thinking about it. My most sincere hope is that someone will be able to prove everything I've said wrong and then write their own book about it that I can read and learn from. I hope that person is you.

If you found this book edifying at all then please share it with your friends and family. If they can't take away something useful from this book that will make their lives and this world a better place then at least one of them might be the person to disprove my flawed theories and save everyone else who may have otherwise been led astray by them.